TWENTIETH-CENTURY

DRAMA

Bamber Gascoigne

HUTCHINSON UNIVERSITY LIBRARY
LONDON

Hutchinson & Co (Publishers) Ltd
3 Fitzroy Square, London W1

London Melbourne Sydney Auckland
Wellington Johannesburg Cape Town
and agencies throughout the world

First published 1962
Reprinted 1962, 1963, 1965, 1967, 1970, 1974

Printed in Great Britain by litho on smooth wove paper
by Anchor Press, and bound by Wm. Brendon,
both of Tiptree, Essex

ISBN 0 09 065842 6 (cased)
0 09 065843 4 (paper)

Contents

CONTENTS

Preface

Ibsen is often called the 'father of modern drama', but contemporary drama can more properly be said to begin with
Pirandello. Various reasons make this so. The first nights of his
plays (*Six Characters*, for example, appeared in 1921) are well within living memory; he has probably had more influence on the
theatre of the last forty years than any other single dramatist;
and audiences still go to his plays under the impression that
they are patronizing the *avant-garde*, whereas the works of Ibsen,
Chekhov, Shaw and even perhaps Strindberg have all by now
achieved the status of classics. This book, therefore, is a study of
Western drama in the four decades since Pirandello became a
playwright of international standing.

Before embarking on a study of modern theatre one needs
to clarify two much-misused terms: 'naturalism' and 'realism'.
The meaning of 'naturalism' is beyond dispute—it represents a
style of theatre in which the stage-setting, the dialogue of the
characters and the performance of the actors seem 'life-like'—
but 'realism' is often pressed into service as a synonym for it.
This is confusing and wasteful. I prefer to make the distinction
that naturalism is a description of style and realism of content.
Naturalism reflects accurately the surface of life, whereas
realism is concerned with the truth of the experience which it
conveys. Thus the two are compatible but not inseparable. The
alternatives to naturalism become expressionism, poetic drama,
etc., and the alternatives to realism are fantasy or melodrama.
In this book I have used 'naturalism' for the style itself and
'Naturalism' for the aesthetic movement made famous by
Zola in the 1870's, though in fact anticipated about ten years
earlier in England by Tom Robertson.

Dates of plays are given in the index and are mentioned in
the text only where they are relevant to the argument. Trans-
lations, unless otherwise credited, are my own.

Amongst those who have made this book possible my thanks are chiefly due to the Commonwealth Fund for a Harkness Fellowship with which I was able to study theatre in America for a year; to a bashful friend at Cambridge for reading the typescript and for suggesting many alterations and improvements; and to Christina Ditchburn for providing encouragement and criticism in the right proportions and, even more important, at the right moments.

Acknowledgments are due to the following for permission to quote extracts from copyright material: Allen & Unwin Ltd, *The Dramatic Works of John M. Synge*; The Bodley Head Ltd, *The Eve of St Mark* by Maxwell Anderson, *Air Raid* by Archibald Macleish, 'The Machine Wreckers' and 'Transfiguration' in *Seven Plays* by Ernst Toller; Jonathan Cape Ltd, *Long Day's Journey into Night* by Eugene O'Neill, *The Wesker Trilogy* by Arnold Wesker; Constable & Co Ltd, *The Garbage Man* by John Dos Passos; Dennis Dobson, *What is Theatre?* by Eric Bentley; Editions Gallimard, *L'Etat de Siège* and *Les Justes* by Albert Camus; Editions Bernard Grasset, *Théâtre* by Jean Giraudoux; Editions de la Table Ronde, *Pièces Noires* and *Nouvelles Pièces Noires* by Jean Anouilh; Eyre & Spottiswoode Ltd, *Brecht, a Choice of Evils* by Martin Esslin; Faber & Faber Ltd, *Waiting for Godot* by Samuel Beckett, *The Cocktail Party*, *The Elder Statesman*, *Family Reunion*, *Murder in the Cathedral* and *Collected Poems* by T. S. Eliot; Hamish Hamilton Ltd, *Thunder Rock* by Robert Ardrey; Harvard University Press, *This Music Crept by Me on the Waters* by Archibald Macleish; Houghton Mifflin Co, *Panic* by Archibald Macleish; Indiana University Press, *The Age of Pirandello* by Lander MacClintock; Macmillan & Co Ltd, 'Shadow of a Gunman' and 'The Silver Tassie' in *Collected Plays* by Sean O'Casey; M.C.A. Ltd, 'All My Sons' (© 1947 by Arthur Miller), 'The Crucible' (© 1952, 1953 by Arthur Miller), 'A View from the Bridge' (© 1955, 1957 by Arthur Miller) in *Collected Plays*, Cresset Press Ltd 1958; Methuen & Co Ltd, *The Hostage* by Brendan Behan, *Duel of Angels* and *Tiger at the Gates* by Jean Giraudoux, *A Slight Ache* and *The Caretaker* by Harold Pinter; New Directions, *Three Tragedies* by Lorca; Oxford University Press, 'And so ad Infinitum' by J. and K. Čapek; Putnam & Co Ltd, *Theatre in a Changing Europe* edited by T. Dickinson and *Seven Short Plays* by Lady Gregory; Random House Inc, *Bury the Dead* by Irwin Shaw; Secker & Warburg Ltd, *Plays* by Tennessee Williams; Suhrkamp Verlag, *Die Mutter* by Bertolt Brecht, *Biedermann und die Brandstifter* by Max Frisch; Thames & Hudson Ltd, London, *American Drama since 1918* by J. W. Krutch; University of Minnesota Press, *Parables for the Theatre* by E. and M. Bentley; University of Pennsylvania Press, *The Drama of Luigi Pirandello* by Domenico Vittorini.

Introduction

Memory in the theatre is surprisingly short. This is partly because a production dies almost without trace on the last night of its run, whereas the novels of a decade ago are still on our shelves; but there is also the fact that, after eighty years in pursuit of Originality, the *avant-garde* cannot afford to look behind itself. Rather than risk not seeming new, it still boasts of having just knocked down that hoariest of Aunt Sallies, the well-made play. So André Barsacq, a genuinely distinguished French designer and director, was able to say in 1960 of French post-war theatre:

> There seems to be an escape from the unchanging rules which up till now presided over the drama; by which I mean the division into clear-cut acts with an unfolding of the plot and a dénouement. . . . The theatre is trying to throw off the restraints of the conventions in which it existed up to the war, and is, in consequence, enjoying more freedom in the construction of plays, and even in their subject-matter. There are even plays without action, where the plot rests on the confession of a character; *L'Œuf* by Marceau, for instance, is not constructed according to the sacred rules, since departures are made both in time and space; you are continually skipping from one period to another. Personally, I feel this is all to the good, and the public itself seems to find more satisfaction in escaping from the old type of rigid construction.[1]

This is like praising Teddy Boys for having given up top-hats for everyday wear; it merely overlooks the fact that the real Edwardians gave them up fifty years ago. Only slightly less ridiculous is Arthur Miller's claim that *Death of a Salesman* 'broke the bounds . . . of a long convention of realism'.[2]

I am not suggesting that André Barsacq is quite unaware of the huge variety of theatrical experiment that has been going on since the beginning of this century. His remarks were made only in an interview and, if challenged, he would qualify them. But that they could have been made at all today, however casually, suggests a prevalent belief—and most of us would admit that we share it to some degree—that it is new and daring to be 'theatrical' in the theatre. In fact, the 'unchanging rules', 'the division into clear-cut acts with an unfolding of the plot and a dénouement' and the 'old type of rigid construction' have not been the norm since the great days of Scribe and Sardou; and the reaction against them came before 1890. Admittedly, the majority of Ibsen's plays are 'well made' (though his reputation for naturalness and brilliance of construction belittles him), and it is his prominence that has made the three-act domestic play seem normal. He is the father figure against whom we are proud to rebel. But he did die in 1906. And even before his death Strindberg had written *The Dream Play* (1902), which shows no more respect for considerations of time and place than do our dreams.

Seen in perspective the theatre of the nineteen-forties and fifties is conservative. It is the period from 1880 to 1930 that theatre historians of the future will regard as the age of experiment, the true hey-day of *avant-gardisme*. In those years the bounds of the theatre were stretched to their utmost limits, and sometimes beyond. However ridiculous the result, theory was carried to the extreme in every direction. The microscopic was reached in a play of Austin Strong's in which the stage represented the inside of a man's skull (*Play without a Name*), and the macroscopic in dramas of social revolution, such as Hauptmann's *The Weavers*, where an entire class is the protagonist. Čapek's *Adam the Creator* and Shaw's *Back to Methuselah* both spanned the whole of mankind's development; the action of Salacrou's *The Unknown Girl of Arras* covered one hundredth of a second, the time it takes a bullet to travel from a suicide's pistol to his brain. Strindberg and Cocteau wrote plays with only one speaking character; the Russians and the Germans put on mass dramas with casts of anything up to eight thousand

The expressionists were using fantastic means to portray the crazy logic of men's souls, while the Naturalists, concerned with the outer semblance of reality, became so distressed by the problem of the non-existent fourth wall that one director tried to improve matters by laying a fender and fire-tongs against the footlights. Yeats wanted his verse plays to be performed on a rug at one end of an ordinary room; Reinhardt produced a modern version of *Everyman* on the steps of Salzburg Cathedral and on such a colossal scale that he had actors placed in the towers of all the surrounding churches, one of them so far away that his cry arrived five seconds after the others. Gordon Craig was pleading for pure beauty in the theatre, while the Mechanists wanted only machinery, even dressing the human body up to look like a machine and at times doing away with actors altogether in favour of electrically moved figures. The Dadaists invented a form of theatre which included throwing things at the audience.

The profusion of 'isms' reflects this turmoil—Expressionism, Impressionism, Symbolism, Theatricalism, Naturalism, Mechanism, Futurism, Dadaism, Formalism, Constructivism, Functionalism—and it is not surprising that amongst so much activity almost everything was tried at least once. So, for example, theatre-in-the-round, or 'arena theatre' as it is called in America, which is the great hope of some people in the theatre today, was already old hat in the twenties when Brecht's plays were often performed in boxing rings—and it could anyway never claim any startling degree of originality when set beside an idea like Gropius's in Vienna in 1924 of having a revolving audience surrounded by a ring of stages and film screens. In the same way the theatrical paradoxes which we think of as being Pirandello's chief claim to originality had been developed before him by two Russians, Evreinov and Andreyev; Genet's dedicated undermining of conventional morality follows in a direct line from Wedekind and Rimbaud; and Ionesco's parrot-like bourgeois monsters were on the stage in full force in Cocteau's *The Bridal Pair of the Eiffel Tower* in 1921—if not before.

This is not to disparage theatre-in-the-round, Pirandello,

Genet or Ionesco but to discredit the idea of Originality, on which we put such value. To begin with, it is a quality which it is almost impossible to assess without a most profound knowledge of the whole world's literature. It is also, in the sense in which we commonly use the word, a quality of very doubtful value. The only true originality lies in the uniqueness of an individual artist's attitude to the world and to his experience. If he is a great artist, and his work is true to his experience, then his work will share this uniqueness and will be genuinely 'original'. But this type of originality is rarely recognized by contemporaries. The originality that we do recognize is something more superficial and something that does not last. So Ibsen's contemporaries felt that his originality lay in his daring choice of subject-matter. Sixty years later this aspect of his work—the 'problem' part of his problem-plays—is the one great obstacle to enjoyment of the plays. Strindberg is now admired for his 'conventional' pieces, not for his experimental fantasies. I would go so far as to say that but for the merits of *Miss Julie* and *The Father*, *The Dream Play* and *The Ghost Sonata* would now be totally forgotten by everyone except source-spotting theatre historians. In the same way Pirandello would not have survived if his merit had been confined to his so-called originality—which, by itself, amounts to little more than intellectual gymnastics. To give one example on the other side, Jean Cocteau is a talented artist who seems to cry out for the label 'original'. Almost every play of his has been a totally new experiment (in extreme contrast to Shakespeare, whose whole life's work was one long and slowly developing experiment). As a result Cocteau's plays form no sort of a whole, his work shows no sign of a personal force behind it. And his plays will not, I think, last.

It is this question of what will last—by which I mean what will always be interesting even if not admirable—which has been my main criterion in this book. Looking back over the history of the theatre, there are two distinct groups of plays which do last. The first consists of the work of the few really good dramatists, however isolated those dramatists may be; and the second of plays which form part of a trend in playwriting which, however worthless, was unique in a particular time or place. An example of the first is Georg Büchner, who stands alone and magnificent in the early nineteenth century on the strength of only one or two plays—and of the second the Sentimental Comedies of Augustan and early Georgian England. The lesser playwrights who are not fortunate enough to be part of a school or trend are soon forgotten.

These considerations have also dictated the shape of the book. It is in three parts. The first two deal with the main trends in drama since the First World War; Part One in terms of *Subject-matter* and Part Two of *Style*. The third Part consists of separate studies of the leading dramatists of the period. The man who suffers from neglect by this scheme is the minor playwright who stands outside the main trends, but then, as I have just suggested, he is a creature doomed to early oblivion without my help.

Subject-matter I have treated chronologically. Contemporary drama has reflected very closely the changing atmosphere in Europe and America over the last forty years, and I have tried to relate the main body of serious plays at any one time to their particular background. For this purpose the period falls neatly into four decades, each very different in character—the hectic boom twenties, the depression, the Second World War and the new prosperity in the nuclear fifties.

Even an 'exhaustive survey', which this book is not, can never give a complete picture of such a wide subject as forty years of Western drama, and my section on *Style* lays even less claim to doing so than the one on *Subject-matter*. (Readers who want a very full survey of the period should consult the last part of Allardyce Nicoll's *World Drama*.) Dramatic style has recently been so diverse that most of the experiments are soon forgotten. In Paris in the late twenties, for example, it seemed that the style of Jean-Jacques Bernard would have a profound influence on modern drama. His theatre was based on the dramatic possibilities inherent in the gaps between bits of dialogue and was known as 'the theatre of silence'. It has since been almost entirely forgotten and this book adds nothing to its memory. I have instead tried to explore the stylistic developments which seem to have been both peculiar to this century and most

widespread in their influence. The three that I have chosen
underlie, I believe, the creative approach of many contemporary playwrights, even if unconsciously, in a way that considerations of how much naturalism is possible or how well
made a play need be certainly no longer do. They occupy a
chapter each, headed: *Towards a poetic drama, The use of symbols* and
In search of significance.

Readers may be surprised, in the chapters on the various
decades, at the failure of certain dramatists to make much of
an appearance; Pirandello, O'Neill and Lorca all pass almost
unnoticed in this section of the book. The reason is that in
dealing with *Subject-matter* I have discussed plays according to how
typical they are and not in terms of their aesthetic merit. It is
frequently the second rank of serious dramatists who are most
typical of their time.

Of course, to disregard aesthetic standards of comparison is
a dangerous activity which, if carried too far, can lead directly
to the ludicrous. I hope I have avoided carrying it too far. I have
kept in mind as a *caveat* the example of a critic who was writing
enthusiastically in the thirties about Russian theatre and who
did let himself get carried away by his thesis. Comparing the
Moscow Art Theatre before and after the Revolution, he
pronounced:

> Nothing has been changed in the Moscow Art Theatre
> but the points of view of its theorizers. . . . Where the
> repertory was formerly made up of Chekhov, Turgeniev,
> A. Tolstoi, Hauptmann, Ibsen and Shakespeare, we now
> have Afinogenov, Kirshon, Olescha, Leonov and Bulgakov.[3]

PART ONE

Subject-Matter

I

The Twenties

*'It was characteristic of the Jazz Age that it
had no interest in politics at all.'*
SCOTT FITZGERALD

THE post-war generation had every reason to be disillusioned.
The 'war to end war' had been pointless and agonizing, and did
not even seem to have made war any less likely once the terms
of the Treaty of Versailles had been announced. To the radicals'
amazement and disgust the old system of unrestrained capitalism appeared to have survived the explosion in every country
except Russia. So the abuses and excesses (excesses both of
wealth and of poverty), which the war effort had temporarily
swept away, would soon be reappearing. German radicals,
including the playwright Ernst Toller, were in gaol for their
part in the Munich uprising of 1919. Their American counter-
parts had high hopes of some degree of socialism from Woodrow
Wilson, but by 1920 the Republican Harding had become President
and big business was given its head. Unprecedented prosperity
soon appeared. The intellectuals were like a doctor longing to
operate on the patient, while the obstinate patient grew, to all
appearances, more and more healthy.

If the world felt like a wilderness, the reaction of those who
could afford it was to 'have themselves a ball'. The result was the
Jazz Age, the vicious whirling of the Bright Young People,
hectically gay to cover up the emptiness. The Charleston was
the best answer to the Waste Land. Some of the writers joined
in, others stood back and derided. Either way, with the positive
values untenable or inapplicable, the inevitable result was satire.
The satire of the participants (Evelyn Waugh, Noël Coward, etc.)
was tinged with admiration for their characters. Others, such as

Aldous Huxley, John Dos Passos or Ernst Toller, quite plainly hated all they saw.

In the theatre the targets of the satire covered the whole range of life, from politicians and armament kings, through the claustrophobic families on Main Street, and all the way down to Mr Zero, the unheroic hero of Elmer Rice's *The Adding Machine* (1923). The keynote is chaos. The characters are dummies rather than people. They rarely have names of their own, but are called The Engineer, Number 5, or Six Hundred Pounds of Passionate Pulchritude. It seemed more pleasant to shock than to please. This was the age of Dadaism; one dada poem consisted of sixty lines, each line of ten words and every word *Damn*! In E. E. Cummings's *Him* (1927) a character 'vomits copiously' in the hero's lap and a woman carries a severed male organ on to the stage, represented by a banana in a blood-stained napkin. In Brecht's *Baal* (1918) two characters, Bolleboll and Gougou, after playing cards for their souls, wander on to the stage, decide it's a good place to pass water and do so. Cocteau's Orpheus (1926) announces:

> We must throw a bomb. We must create a scandal. We need one of those storms that clear the air. It's stifling. One can't breathe any more.

and Elyot, in Noël Coward's *Private Lives* (1930), says:

> Let's blow trumpets, and enjoy the party as much as we can, like very small, quite idiotic school-children.

In Gide's *Oedipus* (1930) the younger generation is described as seeking 'an approval for indecency', though this was very much the older generation's viewpoint. Most of the young rebels would have been deeply shocked if their indecencies had been approved of.

These examples are extreme, but the impression they give—of violence, disgust and disillusion—is a fair one. The pitfall of this mood in art is that it encourages hysteria and melodrama. This was particularly true of the German Expressionists Georg Kaiser and Ernst Toller.

Expressionism had been developed by Strindberg as a method of representing states of mind. In his efforts to cut below the surface he used startling symbols and unrealistic patterns of speech, and dispensed with the logical sequence of time, place and action—with 'consequence', in fact. To later dramatists the freedom and fantasy of this method made it seem ideal for satire. (Such satire was new in the theatre, though not in literature—Swift's work would have had a contemporary ring in the twenties.) Strange contrasts could be used to make telling satirical points. Top-hatted financiers in Toller's *Masses and Man* (1919) haggle in a quite normal way over the price of shares— the only unusual aspect is that the shares are in Guilt, for the war which they are deliberately prolonging. In the same way Karel Čapek's Ant Leaders in *The Insect Play* (1923) gabble a staccato mixture of military commands and pious sentiments which successfully lays bare the hypocrisy of political cant.

Often, however, the freedom of the style proved too much for these dramatists. With the need for surface realism gone, a line or two would be enough to score a point and the satirical net could be stretched infinitely wide. Toller was unable to resist the temptation. In his *Hoppla, We're Alive* (1927) a young waiter rushes on to the stage for the sole purpose of complaining that an old gentleman keeps pinching his bottom. In *Transfiguration* (1917) a woman staggers in to prove in a gory speech that love is just lust, and then reels off again. She is followed by an invalid, whose curt message is that voluntary universal suicide is the only hope. Determined to prove that the misery he presents is typical, Toller shows a hotel porter (in *Hoppla* again) committing suicide because his chosen horse fails to win; he shouts out, as he stabs himself, that he is 'normal, normal!' 'Absolutely normal,' comments a psychiatrist.

Drunk with their freedom from surface reality, the dramatists were forgetting that there had to be an inner reality to make their work anything but rank melodrama. Kaiser in *Gas* (1920) shows an officer who has almost been persuaded to resign his futile commission and to work for the good of humanity. The scene reads:

Enter the officer in extreme perturbation. He unbuckles his sword and is about to lay it on the table. Then he halts and feverishly buckles it on again.

Officer: I—cannot—do—it—I—cannot!

He draws a revolver, places it against his breast, stalks slowly out, step by step. As the door closes, a shot is heard.

The Billionaire's Son, *rising, staring towards the door*: The world is out of joint. Let others force it back again!

(end of scene)[4]

Almost equally unmoving is the moment in Toller's *The Machine Wreckers* (1923) when, in the middle of a conversation about rebellion, a hungry baby cries. His mother runs over to him, and says:

The babe! The babe! O God in Heaven, my babe is in a fit! He's dead.[5]

The positive values of these two dramatists were no less unreal. The same hysterical approach made their message as naïve as their tragedy was melodramatic. In *Transfiguration* the messianic hero tells a huge crowd:

You could go forward with winged feet, while today wherever you go you trail after you iron chains. Oh, if only you were men and women—men and women unqualified —free men and women!

The crowd break down and weep.

A youth: To think that we ever forgot! We are men, men and women!
All: We are men and women![6]

In similar vein, Kaiser's Billionaire's Son is determined that man must renounce industry and go back to agricultural village life. 'Be human, human, human!' he shouts:

. . . Tomorrow you shall be free human beings—in all their fulness and unity! Pastures broad and green shall be your new domains. The settlement shall cover the ashes and the wreckage which now cover the land. You are dismissed from bondage and from profit-making. You are settlers—with only simple needs and the highest rewards— you are men—Men![7]

Messianic allusions abound in these plays. The artist and his hero are seen as prophets crying in the wilderness, bringing the glad message of 'rise up and be human' to an unresponsive multitude. The multitude is usually nothing less than the whole of humanity. Cosmic significance is the order of the day. So Čapek's *Adam the Creator* (1928) depicts, from a very pessimistic and satirical standpoint, the whole development of human society, concluding that the world's terrible state is an inevitable condition. In André Obey's *Noah* (1930) the family in the ark, and on Mount Ararat afterwards, come to represent the whole of humanity. And the end of Kaiser's *From Morn till Midnight* (1916), just after the hero has committed suicide, reads:

> *He has fallen back with arms outstretched against the cross on the back wall. His husky gasp is like an 'Ecce', his heavy sigh like a 'Homo'. One second later all the lamps explode with a loud report.*
> Policeman: There must be a short circuit in the main.
>
> *(curtain)*[8]

The equivalent American dramatists—Elmer Rice, John Dos Passos, Howard Lawson and, in one or two of his plays, Eugene O'Neill—were more restrained. Instead of a baby dying on the stage, Dos Passos has a refrain chanted by strikers to express the hopeless position of the working classes. 'We work to eat to get the strength to work to eat to get the strength to work to eat to get the strength to work . . .' (*Airways Inc.*, 1928). The bosses object to this refrain on the grounds that it may 'destroy confidence'.

The tone can be fierce without becoming hysterical, as in the same author's play *The Moon is a Gong* (1923):

> A Voice on the Radio: In the best interests of prosperity and business interests dearest to the hearts of all 100 per cent native-born citizens it has been decided by the National Committee of ten thousand Chambers of Commerce . . . that there shall be a list made of all dissenters, knockers, Reds, carping critics, nonchurchgoers, wearers of straw hats out of season, nonFordowners, loafers, discontented persons, readers of foreign languages, divorcees, advocates of free love, the eight-hour day, subversive doctrines.
> The Man in the Panama Hat: Lynch them.

It can also be very funny without losing sight of the disgust. Elmer Rice's Mr Zero (*The Adding Machine*, 1923), who went mad between the horrors of his clerking job and his home life and suddenly murdered his boss, has since been having various adventures in heaven. But the moment comes when he must be returned to earth for another spell, this time to work on the very latest and largest adding machine. Naturally he is reluctant. So the captain up in heaven, knowing what goes in this world of movie stars and advertisements, invents a beautiful blonde who is to go down with him. He points to an empty space and describes her standing there, waiting for Mr Zero. At first Mr Zero fails to see her—understandably, since she does not exist. The captain describes her in more detail. Suddenly Mr Zero can see her.

> Zero: Oh sure! Now I see her! What's the matter with me anyhow? Say, she's some jane! Oh, you baby vamp!
> Captain: She'll make you forget your troubles.
> Zero: What troubles are you talking about?

The moment is made more pathetic, and the author's disgust more clear, when one knows that Zero's sex life on earth has been confined to peeping through a blind at a prostitute undressing.

Where there is a positive value in these plays it is, wisely, much vaguer than the Germans'. In *The Moon is a Gong* the ideal of the young hero is to ring the gong of the moon. His destination beyond that action is simply 'somewhere very high . . . where the wind is sheer whiteness'. They are outward-looking plays and the individual, like Swift's Gulliver, is usually just a touchstone for showing up the society around him. Even the sacred cows of the left wing during the next decade, such as the working classes and Marxism, were at this time undercut by cynicism; but then there was, as yet, none of the black-and-white clarity of the issues of the thirties. During this period, for example, the trades unions in the States were busy keeping out the poorer workers for fear of being too closely associated with the labouring classes. In John Howard Lawson's *Processional* (1925) a group of workers capture a Ku Klux Klanman, dressed in his white sheet. They strip him and find he is the old negro Rastus, well known to them all.

Philpotts: You can't belong to the Klan.
Rastus: How come? Anybuddy own a sheet can belong. I reckoned it was safer . . .
Psinski: You ain't fit to associate with class-conscious workmen.

It has often been suggested that the fantastic enthusiasm caused by Lindbergh's flight across the Atlantic in 1927 is a measure of how much any acceptable form of idealism was lacking in the twenties. Here at last was an act of heroism which was entirely admirable. Certainly the plays of the time reflect a disillusion with the more usual forms of heroism. It is rare in the drama of the twenties that a martyrdom is worth while or an apparent magnificence real. In the plays of Dos Passos and of Toller working-class leaders are martyred to no purpose, and Sean O'Casey's warm-hearted farces are set against a background of pointless death in the Easter Rebellion of 1916. It is typical that Minnie, the heroine of *Shadow of a Gunman* (1923), is shot accidentally by her own side. And Seumas says:

I believe in the freedom of Ireland, an' that England has no right to be here, but I draw the line when I hear the gunmen blowin' about dyin' for the people, when it's the people that are dyin' for the gunmen! With all respect for the gunmen, I don't want them to die for me.

To O'Casey it is the characters least puffed-up with heroism who are the heroes. Similarly Cocteau (in *The Infernal Machine*, 1932) reduces mighty Oedipus to a vain figure staggering round the stage as he tries out various ways of carrying the dead body of the sphinx, in this case a jackal—he is looking for the most impressive method to use in his triumphal entry into Thebes. Giraudoux's Judith (*Judith*, 1931) kills Holofernes for love and is then unable to prevent the Jewish chroniclers and priests from celebrating her deed as one of great nationalistic heroism by a frightened virgin. And Robert Emmett Sherwood (in *The Road to Rome*, 1926) confounds the glorious Hannibal simply by making a woman ask him at the gates of Rome: 'You have come all this way, at enormous expense—*Why?*'

An amazed and disapproving *Why?* could be said to be the keynote of the drama of the twenties. It was not a constructive *Why?* since it was rarely followed by suggestions for *How else?* Most of the plays accepted implicitly that there was nothing to be done—certainly nothing specific. It was essentially a theatre of inaction, a negative theatre. Individual plays, of course, stand out as exceptions. One was Shaw's *Saint Joan* (1924) which, amongst so many plays where both sides were wrong, stands as a magnificent example of one where both sides are right. Another was O'Neill's *Desire under the Elms* (1924), bursting with real life at a time when most characters were cardboard-thin. But even Shaw came back to the current feeling with *The Apple Cart* (1929), and O'Neill was guilty of such paper-weight abstractions as *The Great God Brown* (1926) and *Lazarus Laughed* (1928).

In Dos Passos's *The Moon is a Gong* the central couple break out of the materialistic dance of death and describe their position as 'ahead of us the dragon, behind us the pink pig'. The emphasis in the plays of the twenties was almost exclusively on the pink pig. The dragon had been too vague and remote, but from

1928 on it would become more and more clearly defined in the form of the depression. And the type of weapon to hand for slaying it would be the strike weapon, or the weapon of reform. With the depression we move into a theatre of action.

There had, however, been one country where the theatre in the twenties had been most aggressively positive—the Soviet Union, where the pink pig was already dead by 1917 and the dragon was urgently demanding attention. Here theatre was used for the first time in this century as a powerful propaganda weapon. Support for the new régime had to be stimulated throughout the nation, together with the acceptance of bewildering ideas of community. Since the peasants were illiterate, the quickest way of reaching them was through theatre. An organization was formed, under the direction of Meyerhold, which sent groups all over the country to perform plays and to promote local dramatic activity. These groups were literally referred to as 'shock troops' or 'flying brigades'. There were several brilliant directors in Moscow at the time, and plenty of money was made available to them. So, for a while, Russian theatre seemed the most hopeful in the world. But, however much directors and actors may thrive, dramatists can achieve nothing if their writing is made subject to a party policy. Ilya Ehrenburg, in his *Destruction of Europe* (1924), presented the Red Army digging a tunnel from Leningrad to New York and then marching through it to save the world from capitalism. Beside such naïveté Kaiser and Toller come to look like very wise and very moderate old men.

2

The Thirties

'To bring on the revolution, it may be necessary to work within the Communist party.'
SCOTT FITZGERALD

EVER since the *Oresteia*, theatre has been, in the broadest sense, political—it has reflected contemporary affairs. But the 1930's stand out from the whole history of the theatre as *the* decade of political theatre. The propaganda theatre of Russia in the twenties had merely been part of the machinery of government under a dictatorship, and the same use of art would crop up in Hitler's Germany. What was new in the free world in the thirties was the way in which individual authors began to use the stage as a soap-box, from which they could shout their own personal solutions to contemporary problems.

It was the depression which brought about the change. In the boom days the politically minded writers had felt themselves to be voices crying in a spiritual wilderness. Once the wilderness became material as well, and the general public for the first time had to admit that something was wrong, the writers' views began to be listened to. Their views, in turn, became much more specific, because the problems were now specific.

If the ideal had once been to strike the gong of the moon, it was now to organize a strike, and to hell with the moon. The man needed was no longer a Christ-figure—a simple union-organizer would do much better. People in the twenties had been urged to be 'human'. Now, when millions were reduced by poverty and unemployment to an animal level of existence, it was assumed that they were human and they were urged to act. 'Power is people', concludes Lawson's *Marching Song* (1937).

This change—from a theatre of inaction to one of action, and from the general to the specific—was naturally accompanied by other changes. The majority of the new plays were naturalistic in style. Expressionism and fantasy had been ideal for plays whose sweep took in the whole of humanity and history, but they were unable to do justice to the here and now. The change carried over into the audience too. Plays dealing seriously with economic problems brought into the theatre the people who were directly concerned with those problems. Soon the new audiences were themselves performing the new plays, and in new environments. So Clifford Odets' *Waiting for Lefty* (1935) was often performed by the very people it was about—taxi-drivers at a strike meeting. One of the 'smash hits' of the decade, the revue *Pins and Needles* (1938), was presented by the International Ladies' Garment Workers' Union, and a group called Theatre Union gave free seats for its productions to the unemployed. A part of the American theatre had become a debating platform, where whole sections of the community could put their point of view. The highest peak of political theatre came in America with the excellent Federal Theatre Project, and the lowest depths at about the same time in Germany, with Hitler's terrifying, though highly dramatic, mass rallies.

The change is visible in the work of the individual dramatists who had already achieved prominence. In the twenties Brecht had been writing harsh extravaganzas, which were, perhaps, only three parts satire and one part a sneaking admiration. Toller had treated humanity at large no more kindly or realistically than Hieronimus Bosch, and Karel Čapek had ventured no closer to everyday reality than war on an ant-hill, disaster in a world overrun by robots, the problems of a woman with everlasting life and the difficulties encountered by Adam in populating a totally new planet.

About 1930 Brecht's style changed abruptly, and he started writing cool, didactic pieces which he himself called *Lehrstücke* ('teaching plays'). They dealt with the problems facing individuals who are working for Communism—questions of relative values and practical morality. They were performed in schools and at party meetings. The actors and audience discussed their meaning and in one case a discussion of the ideology behind the play caused Brecht to alter the ending of his plot. In 1936–7—he was by then in exile—he wrote a play which pictured realistically the whole life of Germany under the Nazis and which called for someone to say 'no' to it—*Fear and Misery in the Third Reich*. This play cast its net wide over the whole community, but the soberness with which it presented its scenes of everyday life—housewives queueing up to buy meat, scientists working without freedom of expression, a Jewish wife having to leave her Aryan husband—made it very different from the frenzied panoramas of the twenties.

Meanwhile Toller—also in exile—had, in the face of the appalling events in Germany, lost all his hysteria. He wrote in 1938 *Pastor Hall*, a successful and realistic picture of the final stand against the Nazi régime of a pastor, whose resistance has until then been passive. And Karel Čapek emerged in the same year from ten years' retirement to write a play against the armaments race (*Power and Glory*) and, in 1939, another, in which a mother sends her last son to join the war. This was *The Mother*, and it contains the whole change of attitude from the old days of the twenties, when heroism was extremely suspect. This woman's menfolk have all in the past died heroic but futile deaths— her husband in a ludicrous battle with a native tribe, one son trying to beat the altitude record and two others on opposite sides of the same civil war. Her last son she adamantly keeps at home, until she hears that the enemy in the present war are slaughtering children. She then orders him out to fight.

American dramatists show the same change. Elmer Rice, for example, moved from the expressionistic fantasies of *The Adding Machine* (1923) and *The Subway* (1924), through his realistic picture of New York tenement life, *Street-Scene* (1928), to *We, the People* (1933), an unwieldy great canvas of American life and corruption which is similar in intention, though not in merit, to *Fear and Misery in the Third Reich*. By the mid-thirties almost every aspect of contemporary life was crowding on to the American stage, and indeed a future historian, if all other documents were destroyed, could easily piece together the American history of the time from its plays alone. They fall roughly into three categories, reflecting the three great problems of the decade—the depression, the rise of Fascism and the possibility of another war.

All the aspects of the depression scene, which Elmer Rice had crowded into *We, the People*, were treated rather more effectively one by one by other playwrights. Maxwell Anderson wrote an investigation into the corruptions of Congress in the form of a board-room thriller (*Both your Houses*, 1933). Civil rights were defended by John Wexley in *They Shall Not Die* (1934), which was based on the trial of six negro boys in Scottsboro, Alabama. Strikes were urged on the workers in *Stevedore* (1934) by Peters and Sklar, in *Marching Song* (1937) by John Howard Lawson and in Odets' *Waiting for Lefty* (1935). The mood of these plays is invariably one of optimism. Action is always eventually possible and will be worth while. The strike-organizer is a wholly admirable man, with no doubts to assail him in his work: his worries are confined to the opposition to his plans. He has to contend with the scheming subtlety of the boss, the apathy of some of the workers, the colour-prejudice of others, the treachery of a few more—and always the accusations against himself of being a 'red' and a 'nigger-lover'. Usually he dies in his efforts, shot by outraged whites or framed by the police. But after, and because of him, the good time begins.

Far from being isolationist, American authors were producing anti-Nazi plays before anyone else. Two appeared in 1934, Elmer Rice's *Judgement Day* and S. N. Behrman's *Rain from Heaven*. Clifford Odets' *Till the Day I Die* followed in 1935. There were to be many others, but they are in one sense very different from the equivalent plays written by authors who had lived under the Nazis. There is an element in the American plays of the horrified fascination which was later to move Orwell to write *1984*. *Till the Day I Die* shows, step by step, how a captured Communist can be made to appear to have turned traitor—by, for example, putting him beside the driver of an armoured car which goes to destroy a Communist hide-out. In *Judgement Day* Elmer Rice adapted the facts of the Reichstag Fire Trial so that, in his version, not only are the Communist defendants innocent, but the crime for which they are to be condemned to death has not even happened. It has merely been made to seem to have happened. Both these plays reveal a fascination for the extent to which truth can be distorted under a totalitarian régime, and the criminal subtlety gives them something of the glamour of detective thrillers. It is in this respect that the anti-Nazi plays of Brecht and Toller, both driven into exile by Hitler, seem very different. In *Fear and Misery in the Third Reich* and *Pastor Hall* the snooping and blackmailing by S.S. men is merely sordid.

The largest single group of serious plays was that which dealt with the possibility of another world war. They reflect fairly accurately the changing attitude of America in the second half of the decade.

The year 1936 produced three pacifist plays. Robert Emmet Sherwood in *Idiot's Delight* showed all the worst characteristics emerging in a group of normally civilized and idealistic people as soon as war is declared. Paul Green's *Johnny Johnson* was an expressionistic fantasy about a young idealist's crazy attempts to stop the First World War, which is seen as a gory charade laid on by the generals. For his pains Johnny Johnson spends many years in a lunatic asylum. When he comes out he tries to make a living by selling toys on the street. He fails to do so because he refuses to stock model soldiers, which, once again, have become the only toys in which the children show an interest.

Similar, but even more bitter, was Irwin Shaw's *Bury the Dead*. Six dead soldiers, in an effort to stop the war, refuse to lie down for burial. All the patriotic stops are pulled out by generals and politicians to persuade them to do the right thing by their country, and a priest prays:

> Oh, Jesus . . . give us thy blessing on this holy day, and cause it that our soldiers allow themselves to be buried in peace.

A live soldier, digging the grave for them, kills a trench rat and offers it to the sergeant as a little token of Company A's esteem. When the sergeant refuses, the soldier protests:

Ah, sergeant, I'm disappointed. This rat's a fine pedigreed animal—fed only on the choicest young men the United States's turned out in the last twenty years. . . . Notice the heavy, powerful shoulders to this rat, notice the well-covered flanks, notice the round belly—bank clerks, mechanics, society-leaders, farmers . . . good feeding . . .

The better-known war plays of the twenties, such as *Journey's End* and *What Price Glory?*, had tended almost to romanticize war— certainly they had stressed the camaraderie of it. (O'Casey's *The Silver Tassie* was an exception.) But now, with a repeat performance likely only twenty years later, the full disgust that was in Wilfred Owen's war poetry had at last reached the stage. Suitably, the style used was expressionism—back to the anti-action satirical style of the twenties.

Soon the picture was changing, as the horror and the full intentions of Nazi Germany became more and more apparent. Liberalism, the loving mother of inaction, had for years been a target of T. S. Eliot and others. After Munich it would become anathema to a growing majority in the Western world. Archibald Macleish attacked it in two very effective radio plays, *The Fall of a City* (1937) and *Air Raid* (1938). The former showed a city falling to a dictator simply by appeasing him, by refusing to believe in the reality of his threats and by having no positive way of life to set against his. In *Air Raid* enemy planes are flying towards a European town. The women refuse to be flustered. They know that wars come and go, leaving nothing worse than a few unwanted pregnancies. Beside their calm the men's urgent bustle of preparation is made to seem fairly ridiculous. Then a plane dives. The women, in a sudden panic, rush out into the street, shouting:

> Show it our skirts; it won't hurt us!
> Show it our softness! Show it our weakness!
> Show it our womanhood! Into the street!
> Into the street! All of us!

They are all shot by the machine-guns.

After this the plays suddenly become full of the value of Americanism, of certainty and of resolve. The hero of Robert Ardrey's *Thunder Rock* (1939) is a man who, disgusted by the world situation, has retired to live in a lighthouse. Various events there give him a new perspective on history and he emerges at the end to fight, saying:

A new order that will eradicate oppression, unemployment, starvation and wars as the old order eradicated plague and pestilences . . . That is what we've got to fight for and work for . . . not fighting for fighting's sake, but to make a new world of the old.

Maxwell Anderson's *Key Largo* (1939) and *The Eve of St Mark* (1942) both deal with a man who is in charge of a small group of soldiers defending a hill. The hill cannot be held indefinitely, but it could be held for a few more vital hours at a cost of certain death. In each case higher command gives him permission to withdraw. In *Key Largo* he does so and is for ever after haunted by guilt. Three years later, in the very sentimental *Eve of St Mark*, he stays and dies heroically. A Voice on the Radio expresses the new certainty:

Have you noticed that our soldiers almost never talk about the war, almost never discuss our reasons for fighting? I've noticed it. And have you wondered why? I think I know. This is the first war in history where there's no possible argument about who's right and who's wrong. We're fighting for our lives and fighting to keep men free. You can't argue about that.

The play ends with the dead hero's brothers rushing to join up. 'Make a new world, boys,' says their father, too old to enlist; 'God knows we need it.' A play like Thornton Wilder's *Our Town* (1938), which quietly revels in the ordinary pleasures of small-town life, may at first seem right outside this stream. But it is just another aspect of the same new vision of Americanism.

The change from the twenties, and from the appalling families satirized by Elmer Rice and Sinclair Lewis, is complete.

The most amazing progression along these lines of any single dramatist was Robert Emmet Sherwood's. He moved from the anti-heroic *The Road to Rome* (1926), in which the central character says to Hannibal, 'I want you to believe that every sacrifice made in the name of war is wasted', through the pacifist *Idiot's Delight* (1936), to the nationalistic *Abe Lincoln in Illinois* (1938) and finally to *There Shall Be No Night* (1941), a play in which a leading pacifist changes his beliefs and joins the fight. By this time Sherwood himself was a strong and influential interventionist (prior to Pearl Harbour) and he was soon participating actively in politics in the State Department.

Many of these plays sound laughably melodramatic. In a sense they are, but the times were equally so. If melodrama is drama exaggerated beyond all bounds of probability, then these plays are not so clearly melodramatic. No distortion of justice could be more extreme than the twists contrived by the Nazis. It may seem exaggerated now that in Rice's *We, the People* strikers demonstrating outside an American factory should be fired on by the police; but in 1932, when laid-off employees marched to the Ford factory in Detroit to present a petition, several were wounded by police-fire and four killed. If the poverty presented in the plays seems extreme, one has only to remember that people in Chicago used to rummage in the municipal garbage-dump for food, while President Hoover suggested that restaurant owners could help by putting scrapings from the plates into five-gallon cans for distribution to the unemployed. The corruption in Congress in *Both your Houses* is no more fantastic than had been the Harding scandals of 1923, or the misappropriation of relief funds by General Dawes, or Treasurer Mellon's proposal, when the depression was well under way, of tax reliefs which would, it was calculated, have brought more benefit to him personally than to the entire population of Nebraska.

Simplification is a charge more likely to stick than exaggeration. The issues are plainly black and white. The Nazis helped the symbolism by wearing black shirts and for many writers it

B

was the Communists who were pure white beneath their Red flag and could do no wrong. But at a time when political feelings ran so high most issues did seem very clear and simple—from both sides of the question. It is more fair to say that these playwrights were making direct and unprecedented use of highly dramatic contemporary situations. Organizing a union in the South must have been just as violent a matter as the picture of it in *Stevedore*, and the speed with which real events appeared on the stage supports my point. The Sacco-Vanzetti case, the death of the strikers at the Ford factory in Detroit, the misappropriations of General Dawes and the Reichstag Fire Trial, all became subjects of plays within a year of their happening. The Scottsboro trial and John Wexley's play about it, *They Shall Not Die*, both fall within 1934. And the war plays have a similar sense of immediacy. A character in *Idiot's Delight* (as early as 1936) announces:

> France and Italy are at war. England joins France, Germany joins Italy. And that will drag in the Soviet Union and the Japanese Empire and the United States.

And the opening stage direction of Irwin Shaw's *Bury the Dead* (also 1936) announced the time as 'the second year of the war that is to begin tomorrow night'.

The most extreme example of American political drama was the actual marriage of politics and theatre in the Federal Theatre Project. This part of Roosevelt's New Deal was a scheme to provide work for some of the many thousands of unemployed theatre workers. It began in 1936 and within a very short time there were Federal Theatre productions all over the country. The organizers helped to form local groups and also sent productions touring from New York. Money was short and wages were kept to the bare minimum, but the seats never cost more than a dollar and everywhere there was a spirit of improvisation. In a Maine town the visiting company played free and the townspeople cooked them their supper. In Valley, Nebraska, a place with a population of only one thousand, there was an audience of over nine hundred and fifty for the first production—and the town then invited the players to become residents. At its peak the Federal Theatre was employing thirteen thousand people. It had a weekly audience of half a million and a total audience of twenty-five million. Sinclair Lewis's anti-Fascist play *It Can't Happen Here* opened simultaneously in twenty-one cities in 1937. And in New York the Federal Theatre was responsible for three outstanding productions—Eliot's *Murder in the Cathedral* (which no commercial management would touch), and Orson Welles' productions of *Macbeth*—with an all-negro cast—and of *Dr Faustus*. It also developed the Living Newspaper, a highly successful method presenting to the public urgent topical problems, such as Housing or the Power Monopolies, in a telling and comprehensible form.

Unfortunately the end of the Federal Theatre was political too. From the start it had been attacked by the Republicans as part of their general opposition to the New Deal. The film companies also were strongly opposed to the Federal Theatre on the fantastic grounds that it was taking away the audience of this great industry. The actual figures showed that film attendance had dropped by a half per cent, but the *Motion Picture Herald* solemnly warned its readers that Federal Theatre was 'instructing the young that another form of entertainment exists than motion pictures'.[9] Eventually, in 1939, the Republicans in Congress managed to cut off the grant to the Federal Theatre on a charge of 'leftist activity'. The seriousness of the charge can be judged by the fact that an actor was branded a fellow traveller for having helped to serve tea to players of the visiting Moscow Art Theatre; and a congressman asked, after the production of *Dr Faustus*, whether or not this Marlowe was 'a red'. The Federal Theatre had been both the victim and the child of politics.

This chapter has been mainly about America, since it was undoubtedly the centre of the most typical theatre of the thirties. True theatre in Germany came to an end with Hitler's achievement of power in 1933. In England the theatre of the decade was undistinguished. Noël Coward had passed his prime—he had been, above all, a creature of the wild twenties. Stephen Spender's *Trial of a Judge* (1938) dealt topically and fairly successfully with the difficulties of a judge in a totalitarian régime, and the political fantasies of Auden and Isherwood (*The Dog beneath the Skin*, 1935, *The Ascent of F.6.*, 1936 and *On the Frontier*, 1938) were in parts well barbed and amusing, but were more in the satirical expressionist vein of the twenties. Terence Rattigan was launching his career with a very light farce (*French without Tears*, 1936) and J. B. Priestley was unduly impressed (*vide* his introduction to *Three Time Plays*) by his own playing with time sequences in *Dangerous Corner* (1932), *Time and the Conways* and *I Have Been Here Before* (both 1937). Our theatre, in fact, had its too-well-manicured finger a very long way from the pulse of the world situation. Eliot's *Murder in the Cathedral* (1935) stands head and shoulders above these other plays, but looks forward to the theatrical tone of the next decade. It is at its worst when it is specifically reflecting the problems of the thirties—as in the Knights' speeches of self-justification, satirizing totalitarian hokum.

In France the theatre was more flourishing. Giraudoux had written several effective plays, including *Tiger at the Gates* (*La Guerre de Troie n'aura pas Lieu*, 1935), by far the best anti-war play of the decade: and Salacrou and Anouilh were both by 1939 established in their own country as first-class dramatists. But the tradition developed by these three would come to its peak in the plays written in occupied France. Their preoccupations —with innocence trapped in a harsh world, with the rival pulls of attraction between a heroic death and a chair by the fire, and with the moral problems of ends versus means—were to be the main preoccupations of the drama of the forties. The typical theatre of the thirties was about the need for action to deal with the problems of society. The individual was so unimportant in these plays that Rice's *We, the People*, for example, ends without our knowing whether or not the young hero is going to be executed. The curtain comes down on the lawyer's speech which calls on the whole nation to swamp injustice and which thus carries the play on to the broadest political level, where Rice's real interest lies. In Brecht's *Fear and Misery in the Third Reich* there is a new set of characters in each of the twenty-eight scenes—it is a purely social play. And in nearly all these plays, when action is finally taken, when the strike-leader dies or the son goes off to war, it is assumed that the action will be effective and will have proved worth while. The action itself is positive, and that, for the moment, is enough.

With the outbreak of war, the emphasis changes. The nations have now taken the step into action and the individual is caught up in it willy-nilly. From now on the emphasis is on him—and nowhere does his predicament press harder on him than in the drama of occupied France.

3

The Forties

'Nous voilà condamnés à être plus grands que nous-mêmes.'

Dora, in Camus's *Les Justes*

BY THE end of such American plays as *Thunder Rock* the hero had made his decision to act. As the curtain fell, hearts were warmer and the future looked rosy with honest gun-fire. European drama takes over on the following night. The decision still holds but the first flush of enthusiasm has gone. On closer inspection the whole project looks more complicated. The theatre of the forties could be described (pedantically) as an analysis of the implications of action, from the point of view of the agent.

The most obvious question was the relationship between the means and the end. How much evil is justifiable to achieve how much good? This dilemma had already been mulled over for several years in Europe. Brecht, whose position as a Communist in Germany on the eve of the Nazi régime was similar to that of a free European on the eve of the Second World War, had discussed it in his short didactic plays. In *He Who Said Yes* (1930) the question is whether one member of an expedition can be sacrificed to enable the others to get through the mountains with medicine which will help a whole town. In a similar situation in *The Measures Taken* (1930) a young Communist accepts the necessity for his death, since his life is endangering the local movement. His comrades kill him and throw him into a lime-pit. The chorus comments:

> What meanness would you not commit, to
> Stamp out meanness?

38

> If, at last, you could change the world, what
> Would you think yourself too good for?
> Who are you?
> Sink into the mire
> Embrace the butcher, but
> Change the world; it needs it![10]

Charles Morgan treated the same question in a less extreme form in *The Flashing Stream* (1938). His scientist, Ferrers, is a man who is over-determined to keep his hands clean. His life's work is on the verge of being ruined because the government will not continue his grant unless he publicly accepts the blame for the failure of a series of experiments. He is convinced that he is not to blame and he refuses to tell the lie. Eventually his mistress tells it for him, and, after an initial reaction of disgust, he admires her for her strength in having done so. W. H. Auden's Eric, a pacifist who comes to accept the need to fight (in *On the Frontier*, 1938), expresses this general position well when he describes himself as:

> ... sighting my rifle for the necessary wrong.

But how much wrong can be justified as necessary? This is the crux of Camus's *The Just Ones* (1949), which is based on the assassination of the Russian Archduke Serge, uncle of the Tsar, in 1905. Elaborate plans are made to throw a bomb into his carriage at an exact point on the road, but when the moment comes the hero, Kaliayev, refuses to throw it because there are two children in the carriage with him. The revolutionary group splits violently in its reaction to this. The member who appears most passionately dedicated to the cause, Stepan, demands a vote of censure on Kaliayev, arguing that there may well be no other opportunity for the assassination. Kaliayev answers:

> I will not add to living injustice for the sake of a dead justice.

The others back him up.

It is hard to imagine a more ideal existentialist hero than a *maquisard* and the emergence of Jean-Paul Sartre as a playwright is closely bound up with the French wartime situation. Orestes' murder of Clytaemnestra in his first play, *The Flies* (1943), is a direct political action, justifiable only by the effect it will have of freeing the people of Argos from their guilt-ridden impotence. In his *Men without Shadows* (*Morts sans Sepultures*, 1946) a group of resistance workers are in gaol awaiting interrogation and torture by the Nazis. One of them, the brother of the heroine, is only fifteen. He is terrified and will almost certainly give away vital information, so his sister sits by while her colleagues strangle him. And they are right. He would have died anyway, but only after suffering brutal torture and causing great harm. Salacrou's Dédé sums up the paradox in *Nights of Wrath* (1946) when he says:

> I perform the actions of an assassin, precisely because I am convinced that I would be a criminal if I did *not* perform the actions of an assassin.

If the 'necessary evil' was to be morally justifiable, an absolute honesty was essential. There could be no confusion over motives. Another member of the resistance in *Nights of Wrath* says:

> Am I proud of myself? No. Am I ashamed of myself? No. No pride and no shame.

To wallow in feelings of guilt was as bad as to double-think one's way round responsibility. Guilt cripples action. In *The Flies* Zeus and Aegisthus, priest and politician together, keep the people of Argos in submission by fostering a communal sense of guilt over the death of Agamemnon. After the assassination of Aegisthus and Clytaemnestra, Zeus does his utmost to make Orestes and Electra repent for their action, because he knows he need fear only someone who is prepared to stand by what he has done. Electra succumbs, but Orestes insists that he would commit the murders again. He meant his actions and he saves the town.

The other essential aspect of meaning one's actions is to understand the full implication of them. The students in *He Who Said Yes* tell the boy that they have decided he must be left behind on the mountain. Since this means certain death, he insists that they themselves throw him over the cliff. Very much less enthusiastic now about their decision, but accepting that it is still the same one, they do so. Ugo Betti provides a superb image in *The Burnt Flower Bed* (1952) for this false separation of action and responsibility. A politician, Tomaso, has come to the house of the Grand Old Man of his party. It transpires that he has made plans to have the old man assassinated and to make it seem the work of their enemies. When the old man opens his front door he will be shot by a distant marksman. Tomaso explains why he feels no sense of guilt or responsibility for this. The decision was taken a long time ago, he says, as part of an unavoidable stream of events, and nothing that he could now do would stop it happening. His analogy for the gap between the decision and the event is that he has placed the rifleman

> so far away that the shooting will not even be a crime; it will only be a matter of skill; we shall hardly hear the shot.[11]

The ruthless honesty demanded by these playwrights of their characters does not imply callousness. To suffer is an essential part of the complete action. It is *not to suffer* which would be dishonest, or, at the best, incomplete. In Anouilh's plays only the detached people, the ones out of contact with life, avoid suffering. And for Anouilh, as for Sartre, detachment is death. Sartre's Orestes suffers no less than anyone else would the emotional horror of having killed his mother, but this does not make him regret or disown his action. And when Celia, in T. S. Eliot's *The Cocktail Party* (1949), achieves her full self and goes out to become a missionary, Eliot stresses that her dedication will not lessen her suffering in any way. It will instead increase it, because it will lead her to a most violent death.

Nor is there anything romantic about the martyrdom of

these characters. Their suffering is no grand and passionate enlargement of the whole person. Diégo, the hero of Camus's *The Siege* (1948), says of his fight to save the town from the symbolic plague:

> I have become desiccated in this fight. I am no longer a man and it is just that I die.

One's personal life is the price of commitment to the necessary evil. In both of Camus's resistance plays the love-scenes are brutally broken into by the terrible events in the world. In *The Siege* the romance of Diégo and Victoria is constantly interrupted by the groans of the sick and by the tumbrils of corpses rolling past, until their attempts at tenderness become a gruesome farce. In *The Just Ones*, just before Kaliayev goes out to attempt the assassination for the second time, Dora tries to break through to a mood which lovers in normal times could take for granted.

> Dora: Would you love me if I were light and carefree?
> Kaliayev *hesitates, then in a low voice*: I long to say yes to that.
> Dora, *crying out*: Then say yes, my darling, if that's what you think and if that is true. Yes, in the face of justice, yes, in front of misery and a downtrodden people. Yes, yes, I beseech you, in spite of the agony of the children, in spite of those who are hanged and those who are whipped to death . . .
> Kaliayev: Quiet, Dora.
> Dora: No, one must at least once let one's heart speak out. I'm waiting for you to call to me, to *me*, Dora, for you to call to me above this world which is poisoned with injustice . . .
> Kaliayev, *brutally*: Be quiet. My heart dreams of nothing but you. But at this moment I can't afford to tremble.
> Dora, *bewildered*: At this moment? Oh yes, I was forgetting . . .

He goes out, throws his bomb, is imprisoned, tortured and executed. Dora carries on the good work but the play ends with her words (which echo Diégo's in the earlier play): 'Am I still a woman?'

This is the price of the rebels' action, and in *The Siege* the chorus of women voice the most powerful and insidious temptation to acceptance of things as they are:

> In no matter what part of the world and under every master there will always be a ripe fruit that you can reach out and pick, the poor man's wine, and the wood fire beside which one can wait for the troubles to pass . . .

Again, it was the women in Macleish's *Air Raid* who appreciated the value of the mere continuance of life, and laughed at the men's military bustle. Never in literature have the small things of life had such appeal. The chorus in *Murder in the Cathedral* voice their fear of any change in terms of their own precious hearthside pleasures, and in the later plays of Eliot it is the superficial charms of life, the tea-parties and the pleasant gossip, which prevent many of his characters from delving below life's surface—Eliot's version of taking action.

But it is Anouilh who is at once the high priest of small things and their most violent critic. He sees all humanity—with the one exception of his own young and vital heroines—drifting its way through life on a comfortable cushion of minor physical sensations and dreaming of fat girls' thighs. In almost every one of his plays some comfortable middle-aged body expounds very effectively the pleasures of ordinary life. The old Nurse, faced with Medea's death-welcoming romanticism (*Medea*, 1946), pleads:

> Medea, I'm an old woman, I don't want to die! I've followed you, I've given up everything for you. But the world is still full of good things, the sun on the bench at the bus-stop, hot soup at midday, the few coins that one has earned in one's hand, the drop of something which warms you through and through before you go to sleep.

And Creon, trying to convince Antigone that life is worth holding on to (*Antigone*, 1942), says:

. . . life is a book that one likes, it's a child playing at one's
feet, a tool that just fits one's hand, a seat to rest on in front
of the house . . . perhaps, after all, life is happiness.

These testimonies to life are usually all that is needed to
complete the heroine's determination to die, for they represent
compromise and inaction. Medea kicks the Nurse away with
the one word 'Carcass!' and Antigone is scarcely more polite
in her reaction to what she calls Creon's *sale bonheur*—his sordid
happiness. The case is well put and answered in Salacrou's
Nights of Wrath. Bernard, the little man who has tried to be
unaffected by the German occupation, argues: 'Oh, come now!
One still lives, in more or less the same way. And as long as
one's alive, there's always hope.' He is answered by Jean, a
member of the Resistance: 'No. In this unending night there is
hope only in fighting.'

The other great temptation of such a time was to see the
heavy trundling of the political and economic machines as
inevitable processes. It is often presented as such by the
dramatists. In *Tiger at the Gates* (1935) Hector's efforts to prevent the
Trojan war from taking place are doomed to failure, even
though he and Ulysses, two opposing generals neither of whom
wants his country to fight the other, can stand together on a
balcony and reach complete agreement. Ulysses explains:

You are young Hector! It's usual on the eve of every war
for the two leaders of the peoples concerned to meet
privately at some innocent village, on a terrace in a garden
overlooking a lake. And they decide together that war is the
world's worst scourge, and as they watch the rippling
reflections in the water, with magnolia petals dropping on
to their shoulders, they are both of them peace-loving,
modest and friendly. . . They really are exuding peace, and
the world's desire for peace. And when their meeting is over,
they shake hands in a most sincere brotherly fashion, and
turn to smile and wave as they drive away. And the next day
war breaks out. And so it is with us both at this moment. Our
peoples . . . are not expecting us to win a victory over the

inevitable. They have merely given us full powers, isolated
here together, to stand above the catastrophe and taste the
essential brotherhood of enemies. Taste it. It's a rare dish.
Savour it. But that is all. One of the privileges of the great is
to witness catastrophes from a terrace.[12]

The individual can stand back in a moment of lull, behind or
above the relentless political process, but the process will go
on afterwards. Dramatically this hanging fire, this prolonged
pause of stillness before the consummation of the tragedy, can
be extremely effective. The main scene in Anouilh's *Antigone*
is the one in which Creon tries to save Antigone from being
caught up and destroyed by his own law, made for purely sordid
political reasons. 'It's all just a matter of politics . . . it's part of
the trade,' he tells her, trying in desperation to dissuade her
from her obstinacy while the action and her fate hang suspended. He fails and the machine of political necessity swallows
her up. He is, as he tells his son, 'master before the law—not
after'.

There are equivalent scenes in Montherlant's *Queen after
Death* (also 1942). Ferrante is the king of Portugal and Ines is the
secret, and socially unworthy, wife of his son. His advisers insist
that she must be executed, so that a marriage that is profitable
to the state can be arranged. He hesitates because he finds her
straightforward honesty very appealing and also because he is
weary of the whole business of ruling. In their meetings they
become more and more close and honest with each other—two
human beings, trapped and made into mortal 'enemies' by a
system of which they both disapprove. Ferrante, the powerful
king, at last orders her death without even daring to tell her of
his decision. Montherlant, in order to stress this steam-rollering
of the individual by political necessity, at one time considered
making Ferrante lock himself in his chambers in disgust at the
world and then ask his page through the door: 'Do you think I
will soon be declaring war on Alphonse of Aragon?'

The heroines of these two plays, Antigone and Ines, are, in
a more idealized form, the conventional rebels of the forties.
It is their rôle to say 'no'; no to authority, no to compromise, no

to the small temptations of life, no to the crippling idea that injustice is inevitable, no against all the odds and in the face of logic or coercion. They are romantic versions of the resistance workers of Sartre and Camus. But *Queen after Death* also contains another sort of rebel, equally idealistic though rather less dramatic. He is Pedro, Ferrante's son and Ines' husband. He is a homely creature who admits to finding the business of creating a happy family more important than the business of running a state. When his father urges on him his political responsibility as heir to the throne, he replies:

> The destiny of one being matters as much as the destiny of a million; a soul is worth a kingdom.

But Pedro was out of his time. When disaster was on such a scale that it could involve the extermination of six million Jews, a million souls were undeniably more important than one. Like any human being in the war, Pedro himself could not avoid being caught up in the events around him. His pregnant and innocent wife is executed, his father the king soon dies and he is left in control of the political machine which he despises.

Pedro's time would have come after the war. These plays of the forties have been about the predicament of the individual caught up in the great events of the time, about people like Dora 'condamnés à être plus grands que nous mêmes'—condemned to be greater than they really were. The heightened context of war took these characters into situations where they could, if their author's skill had been greater, have achieved true heroic stature. The tragic hero has to be capable of greatness and capable of suffering, two capabilities which are both inherent, for example, in Hamlet's protest:

> The time is out of joint—O cursed spite,
> That ever I was born to set it right!

The heroes of the resistance plays could all echo this sentiment.

Without suffering, the central character becomes a mere

cardboard hero—as he was in the thirties. Without greatness, he will be a creature more of pathos than of tragedy—as he would be in the fifties, when the terrible and demanding events had passed and, as Jimmy Porter so forcefully pointed out, there was nothing left to be great about.

4

The Fifties

There aren't any good, brave causes left.'
Jimmy Porter

AT THE risk of taking pigeon-holing to the high ecstatic extremes of a bureaucrat, one may say that the thirties produced a theatre calling for action, the forties concentrated on the individual caught up in the action and the post-war theatre was left with all the emphasis on the individual because the action, and the need for it, had passed. If anything, the individual's problem was now that of inaction. With no 'good, brave causes left' as a simple outlet for him, he is now pictured by the play-wrights as a creature heavily pressed upon by family ties, by broad social forces and by a nagging sense of futility. The only positive values consistently put forward by the dramatists of the fifties are the individual's own individuality (or integrity) and his relationship with other human beings. More than any other group of plays since the beginning of the century the theatre of the fifties has been, quite simply, about people.

This is what makes it very different from that of the twenties, even though the two decades were in many respects similar. Looking forward from the twenties to the thirties, Dos Passos had said: 'Ahead of us the dragon, behind us the pink pig.' Now, looking back on the forties, Brecht echoed:

The troubles of the mountains lie behind us,
Before us lie the troubles of the plains.[13]

The fifties had brought the wheel full-cycle and the similarities with the twenties are obvious. Both were post-war decades. Both saw unprecedented prosperity—in certain quarters, at any

48

rate. Each had an uneasy sense of being adrift on a sea of consumer goods.

There were corresponding similarities in the theatre. The plays of the fifties once again lack the specifically political settings which during the thirties and forties had become the norm. This is not surprising. The great and immediate problems which had pressed closely enough on the lives of Western people to be made into drama, such as the depression and the German occupation, had now passed. The problems that remained—the Bomb, the cold war, starvation in under-developed countries—were too huge and too remote to be used in the theatre. The settings of the plays therefore become primarily social once more, but this brings us back to the vital difference between the fifties and the twenties. The modern playwright feels himself inside the society he is writing about; the fears and frustrations of his characters are his own, or even if he does not share them he can sympathize with them. In contrast to this, the playwright of the twenties was an excluded and superior person looking from the outside into a world which he hated. His characters were conceived as symbols of society in its decay and they remained gruesome puppets. Nobody could remember Mr Zero or The Billionaire's Son as anything more than ideas, but the characters of the fifties—Willy Loman, Stanley Kowalski, Jimmy Porter, Beatie Bryant, Archie Rice and even the tramps, such as Beckett's philosophical Didi and Pinter's caretaker, Davies—these all live on as real individual creatures. They also have wide significance as representatives of their society, but this remains an overtone of their personal existence.

Elmer Rice's *The Adding Machine* (1923) and Arthur Miller's *The Death of a Salesman* (1949) provide an interesting example of this contrast between the decades. Both plays are about little men who are tiny parts, indeed almost spare parts, of the huge machinery of capitalism. Both men are overwhelmed by their environment. Their attitudes, which are entirely shaped by their materialistic societies, are strongly criticized by their left-wing authors. Yet, in spite of these similarities, the two plays could hardly be more different. The reason is, as their names have already implied, that Willy Loman is a person, whereas Mr Zero is not. (It is possible that the name Loman is meant to suggest 'low man', providing another almost exact parallel with Mr Zero; but, if so, such unobtrusiveness strengthens my point, providing an index of how far the general significance has been pushed back behind the personal. Few people would notice this interior meaning of Loman, and, in any case, one thinks of him primarily as Willy.) Arthur Miller approaches his theme with sympathy and sorrow, Elmer Rice with horror. Miller, in fact, expresses much of the attitude of the fifties when Linda Loman explodes at her sons' callous treatment of their father (they have left him alone at a night-club while they went off with two girls) and insists: 'Attention must be paid to such a person.' Throughout the fifties attention would be paid.

I am using the term 'fifties' loosely, grouping under it any play specifically post-war in spirit. In the war-plays the harm done to personal relationships was part of the price of the necessary action, but already in Miller's *All My Sons* (1947) the emphasis has changed. The enormity of Joe Keller's dishonesty is brought home to him most strongly by the disastrous effect it later has on his family life. It is above all his responsibility as a human being and as a father which he has betrayed. The same theme is central to John Whiting's two plays, *Saint's Day* and *Marching Song*, written in 1948 and 1952, and is admirably expressed in Ugo Betti's *The Burnt Flower Bed* (1952), in which the central character is the politician Giovanni, a man who has always put politics before people until his young son commits suicide—there was nothing to inspire the boy to keep on living in the burnt flower bed which his parents had made of the world. A spiritual void was opening up, as it had in the twenties. These playwrights were crying their protest against it—as was the horrified professor in Priestley's *The Linden Tree* (1947) who discovered four different types of post-war disillusion inside his own family—but their voices of warning grew steadily fainter. After 1952 John Whiting produced nothing for almost ten years. Christopher Fry reduced the theme of personal involvement to a very thin and light 'message', a mere unfelt cliché, in *Venus Observed* (1950), and it lingered on, even more emasculated, in the plays of

Dennis Cannan. The time was too late for warnings, it seemed. The new playwrights, headed by Beckett and Ionesco, were already writing their highly subjective drama from the middle of the void. (The appearance of their 'school' coincides neatly with the wintriest period of the cold war, but too much can be made of coincidence.)

Beckett's *Waiting for Godot* (1952) was one of the very best plays of the decade. Its two tramps, with their boredom, their fear of pain, their shreds of love and hate, are a surprisingly effective version of the whole human condition—a condition for which action is no answer, chiefly because there is no obvious action to be taken, 'nothing to be done'. Čapek in the twenties had sketched a similar canvas (in *Adam the Creator*, 1928) and had come to the same nihilistic conclusion. But his characters were amusing pawns of his satirical disgust. Beckett's are something much deeper. He himself shares their doubts.

Ionesco is even more inside his own neurotic plays than Beckett. Beckett is in his plays as a part of the world; Ionesco as the world's victim. The little man who is almost invariably his central character suffers the most alarming experiences. He is forced to marry a girl with three noses, he is overfed by brutally affectionate relations and officials, a thirty-foot-long corpse grows in his living-room, all his friends turn into rhinoceroses. Similarly alarming events happen to Arthur Adamov's *Professor Taranne* (1953). These plays are dramatizations of the authors' own fears. Their value is that audiences share these fears, thus preventing the plays, however crazy, from being mere freaks.

With these authors goes Jean Genet, the *dramaturge maudit* of modern France. He has carried the theme of one-ness with his audience to an unexpected extreme. One of the mainsprings of his work is his insistence that everyone in bourgeois society is in reality like himself. (This could hardly be further from the conviction of the left-wing playwrights of the twenties.) The surprise is that he regards himself as thieving, deceitful, disloyal, homosexual, sado-masochistic and capable of murder—and this is the way in which the audience is to be like himself. Genet is therefore dismissing all the accepted virtues as so much cant and is offering a straightforward brotherhood of evil as the only possible good in an intrinsically evil world. Beckett and Ionesco submerge themselves in man's misery, doubt and sense of futility: Genet takes the same path to its romantic extreme.

The next wave of fifties' playwrights, coming this time from England, moved out of this mood of pointlessness and despair. They brought back the earlier insistence on personal relationships, but with a slight difference. Instead of personal relationships being the highest value in life (and their neglect for pursuits of lesser value therefore the major disaster), they are now the *only* remaining value. The new playwrights come to them as a refuge from the despair and futility. Emotional involvement, depth of feeling, integrity—these are the fragments which they have shored against their ruins. So Jimmy Porter (*Look Back in Anger*, 1956), whose life is one long frustration, comes to judge other people by how much they feel. In Osborne's next play, *The Entertainer* (1957), the young heroine refuses a happy and easy life in her fiancé's rich world because she decides that she must stay with her own hopeless family. As she says:

> We've only got ourselves. Somehow we've just got to make a go of it. We've only got ourselves.

Her fiancé's crime was in being detached from other people's sufferings. In Wesker's *Chicken Soup with Barley* (1958) Ronnie's mother, clasping her disillusioned son to her, says:

> You hear me, Ronnie? You've got to care, you've got to care or you'll die.

Robert Bolt's *The Tiger and the Horse* (1960) makes precisely the same point about the need for involvement, but it is essentially involvement with individuals, not with causes. And in *A Man for all Seasons* (1960) the same author reveals a concept of personal integrity very different from anything which would have been acceptable in the forties. Sir Thomas More, who is presented as being admirable, is indifferent to the political events of his time, provided that he himself is not compromised by them. He refuses to say anything that is against his conscience, but equally he is content not to voice his opposition to Henry VIII. Similar is Archibald Macleish's hero in *J.B.* (1957), a supposedly modern version of the Book of Job which in fact has very little contemporary relevance, since Macleish has failed to modernize the characters' terms of reference—they respond to a hydrogen war, for example, with an Old Testament conviction that it must be divine retribution on its individual victims. But J.B. himself is very much in the spirit of the fifties when he proclaims, in the words of the Book of Job:

> Till I die
> I will not violate my integrity.

Ten or fifteen years earlier the vital question would have been at what point he should violate it. After all the terrible disasters have rained down on him, J.B. finally concludes that, however bad everything gets, however meaningless, human beings can still love one another. Personal integrity and personal relationships are the only protection from the void.

Arnold Wesker accurately reflected the full change from the thirties in his trilogy about the Kahn family. The first play, *Chicken Soup with Barley* (1958), begins in 1936. The Kahns are busy with anti-Fascist marches, their friends are setting off for the Spanish Civil War, there is general excitement about the future of Socialism. The atmosphere is of optimistic political bustle. The last play of the three, *I'm Talking about Jerusalem* (1960), is set in the late fifties and shows Ada, the Kahns' daughter, and her husband, Dave, in a house in the country. Dave is trying to live by producing hand-made furniture. He explains that he left the city because he saw men becoming dehumanized in the factory where he worked. But here in the country:

> ... that barn'll be my workshop. There I shall work and here, ten yards from me, where I can see and hear them, will be my family. And they will share in my work, and I shall share in their lives. I don't want to be married to strangers. I've seen the city make strangers of husbands and wives, but not me, not me and my wife.

The wide Socialist aspirations of *Chicken Soup with Barley* have been reduced in scope to the community of the family. Organizations and sweeping solutions are as much out of favour as the Hero. It is, in the end, only other people who are valuable.

There are plenty of other examples of this prevalent emphasis on individuals. Montherlant, who during the war wrote political allegories like *Queen after Death*, has since preferred to probe the psychological tension between small numbers of characters—a subject rather better suited to the Proustian form of novel. One of the most successful plays in London in recent years has been Harold Pinter's *The Caretaker* (1960), which concentrates exclusively on the relationship between a tramp and two brothers, with each of whom he tries to ingratiate himself. It takes place in a ramshackle room, and none of the three characters has any noticeable contact with the outside world. Nor do they, unlike Beckett's tramps in *Waiting for Godot*, discuss the eternal questions about the meaning of life. They merely fight about who shall sleep in which bed, or they make plans, or they grumble; and the play's interest comes directly from the way in which they do these things. At its best it is the very essence of naturalistic drama.

Comparable, though very different, is Jack Gelber's *The Connection* (1960). This is a play about drug-addicts. They sit about on the stage, waiting for their 'fix' of heroin and rambling on in excellent naturalistic dialogue. The scenes are given a trick setting which is intended, like the frame of a *trompe l'œil* painting, to make them seem more real. An author, so the fiction goes, has gathered real 'junkies' together and has told them to perform a script of his. When he climbs on to the stage to complain that they are not keeping to his script, the audience is meant to deduce that they must have been chatting impromptu. A photographer who is filming them keeps muttering in amazement: 'That's the way it is. That's the way it really is.' The audience, Gelber hopes, will share this man's credulity. Most audiences will not, since there are many inconsistencies in the fiction, but it is Gelber's intention which is relevant here. 'That's the way it really is' could be taken as a motto for several recent plays. We have been shown the way it really is in Salford, in Stepney, in Liverpool, building a wall, in an undergraduate's bedroom. At its most serious, as in *The Connection*, this style seems an extension of naturalism—it is virtually behaviourism, jottings from a sociologist's notebook. At its lightest it is mere indulgence in local colour. But in either case it tends to rely on its particular setting and to coast along without either plot or thought.

This behaviourism is therefore the extreme of the emphasis on people *per se*. At least a third of Alun Owen's *Progress to the Park* (1960) was taken up with four young men loafing about in the way that young men do loaf about. This may seem a very free form of theatre, but it is in fact extremely limited. People are much the same in different places, and exceptional groups, such as the drug-addicts, are usually more suitable material for a documentary.

The drama of the sixties will have to turn away from this behaviourist extreme. I suspect and hope that the direction it will take will be towards something crisper, something more intelligent, something more concerned with moral questions; something, in fact, more like the work of Eric Bentley's ideal—the playwright as thinker.

PART TWO

Style

5

Towards a Poetic Drama

POETS have always wanted to write plays and playwrights have
been haunted by the feeling that their dramas would be better
if they were poetic. The argument is that dramatic characters
must be larger than life and, in the same way, dramatic language
must be something higher than the prose which Molière's
Bourgeois Gentilhomme talked without knowing it. Some have
carried this attitude so far as to maintain that there can be no
real drama except poetic drama.

Unfortunately, to many people poetic drama means something Shakespearian, and the most serious charge that Shakespeare
will have to face on the day of judgement will be the dramatic
output of his imitators. His rich language and the iambic line
form a poetic cobweb which has stifled dramatists for three
hundred years, and continues to do so. When I was at a drama
school in America a student wrote a poetic play which was
much admired. It was set in the American Civil War. In it a
Yankee officer said of his heroic son:

> For he did die most royally, the boy.

The same synthetic beauty still pervades many professional
plays. Often in the theatre one's first intimation that a new
play is in verse is the way in which the sentences go *te-thump*ing
on past the end of their meaning to the end of the iambic line.
The average theatre-goer, noticing the 'poetry' without finding
it ridiculous, is quite likely to respond. So, it seems, are some
of the critics. Several profess to find *Elizabeth the Queen* (1930) one
of Maxwell Anderson's best plays. In it he has taken the
Elizabethan language, rhythm, style and subject-matter but has
left behind the Elizabethan virility. His play, though full of good
craftsmanship, is just a sentimental tragedy, more worthy of the

59

early eighteenth century than the sixteenth or the twentieth. Elizabeth and Essex, in spite of their terrible deeds, remain essentially 'lovely people'.

A play like this is neither reproduction nor adaptation—it has neither the value of a Van Meegeren 'Vermeer' nor of a Picasso re-working of Velasquez or Rembrandt. It is merely an exercise in poeticism. In England the same thing was being done by Laurence Binyon and by Gordon Bottomley, who wrote a series of Scottish Shakespearian plays which can best be described as the bastards of Macbeth's dotage. In his later plays Bottomley stirred in, for good measure, elements of Nō theatre. The results were technically interesting but were too esoteric to be anything more. Since then an American, Paul Goodman, has achieved the remarkable feat of writing a formally perfect Nō play (*Stop Light*), of which the subject is a traffic accident.

This type of academic grafting (after all, *Stop Light* could be said to be 'combining tradition with modern reality', though it would discredit the concept for ever) was clearly not the way towards a modern poetic theatre. Nor was that of poets like Claudel and Yeats, who wrote their poetry in dramatic form without paying sufficient attention to the demands of the theatre. This was not true of all their plays, but of the majority. Yeats's *The Shadowy Waters* (1911) is more at home in the collected volume of his poetry than with his plays; and Claudel's *The Midday Break* and *The Satin Slipper* (written 1906 and 1922) will, after a brief vogue, go the way of Shelley's *The Cenci*—remembered but unperformed.

What, then, was to be the way? Any discussion of it must start with Eliot, because in his poetry, already very dramatic in form, he provided two verse styles which much modern poetic drama has since made use of. He introduced the obsessive repetition of:

> 'What is that noise?'
> > The wind under the door.
> 'What is that noise now? What is the wind doing?'
> > Nothing again nothing.

'Do
'You know nothing. Do you see nothing? Do you remember
Nothing?'

(*The Waste Land*, 1922)

and, more important, the clarity and odd formality of:

But there was no information, and so we continued
And arrived at evening, not a moment too soon
Finding the place; it was (you may say) satisfactory.

(*Journey of the Magi*, 1927)

One of Eliot's main achievements was in bringing back ordinary
prosaic words into poetry—not just the rich lower-class words
which have a romance of their own, but the routine admin-
istrative middle-class words which would seem to be the
antithesis of poetry. 'Satisfactory' is just such a word, but in
context it is superb. This quality of unadorned directness has
had a wide and excellent influence on modern dramatic poetry.
To recognize its value one has only to compare the tough clarity
of a good modern translation of a Greek tragedy (such as Philip
Vellacott's *Oresteia* in the Penguin edition) with the fanciful
flights of Gilbert Murray and his Victorian predecessors.

When Eliot himself started writing plays he rejected the
iambic line because the nineteenth century had made it so
noticeably 'poetic'. He decided instead to use a wide variety of
different rhythms and styles of modern verse because he
believed that the poetry should be not just an added delight for
a cultivated audience, or a side-dish to the play proper, but,
instead, a sensitive controller of the audience's reaction. On the
other side of the Atlantic Archibald Macleish was rejecting the
iambic line for a slightly different reason. Its rhythm, he said,
was that of an upbeat, whereas ordinary American speech
tended to fall away in downbeats. But Eliot and Macleish were
alike in their determination to find a poetic drama that was real
for the twentieth century.

Eliot's first play, *Murder in the Cathedral* (1935), turned out to be
both the starting point and the peak of the attempt to use
modern poetry as the language of drama. He achieved nearly

all his aims in this play. The language seemed honest and natural to the characters, while the rhythms reflected very closely the changes of mood. Examples can be found throughout the play, but I quote a passage in which the chorus tell of the small things of their everyday life and then of the new fear that has come to them. The change is obvious and right.

> We have seen births, deaths and marriages,
> We have had various scandals,
> We have had laughter and gossip,
> Several girls have disappeared
> Unaccountably, and some not able to.
> We have all had our private terrors,
> Our particular shadows, our secret fears.
> But now a great fear is upon us, a fear not of one
>   but of many,
> A fear like birth and death, when we see birth and
>   death alone
> In a void apart. We
> Are afraid in a fear which we cannot know, which we
>   cannot face, which none understands,
> And our hearts are torn from us, our brains unskinned
>   like the layers of an onion, our selves are lost lost
> In a final fear which none understands.

At one point in this play Eliot uses a rhyming couplet to suggest perfectly the superficiality of the First Tempter; elsewhere he is able with another sort of rhyming couplet to give a directly opposite impression—that of Thomas's deep new calm. With this new and varied dramatic verse anything must have seemed possible. But *Murder in the Cathedral* was a special case. It was a pageant-play; it was set far away in another time; and it included, quite naturally, a chorus, in the form of the people of Canterbury. It was when Eliot himself and other dramatists tried to extend the range of this dramatic poetry that the difficulties appeared.

Auden, Spender and Macleish were capable of achieving effects as good as Eliot's with varied rhythms and rhymes, but the poetry became a more awkward servant once they tried to move the setting from the twelfth century to the twentieth. It is quite acceptable that Thomas and the Tempters and the people of Canterbury should make pronouncements rather than talk to one another—the play is after all, more than anything else, a debate on morals—but it seems rather odd when Macleish's bankers in *Panic* (1936), faced by the crash of 1928, say:

What can we fight?
    What can we see?
    What can we
See to fight?
    Nothing to fight against.
          No one—there's
No one. There's nothing.
      Fighting the fog.
        Fighting the
Fall of the night and there's nothing.
        No one against us.
No one!
The dead stacks; the black dust; the
Rust on the tracks and there's no one.
      The silence in valleys,
The factories lightless at dusk by the sidings;
  the couplings
Loose in the yards and no one; there's nothing.
Riders on Rods and on roads and by water and running
  away and from
No one; the loads in the Fords and from far and
  from no one
Running away from it . . .

In this the bankers are partly chanting as a chorus, partly reciting a piece of impressionistic modern poetry; neither of which activities is particularly close to the reality of the modern banker's existence. The problem was that if modern characters converse in poetry one loses all sense of realism, while if they converse realistically one loses all sense of poetry, as in these lines from one of Macleish's radio plays:

> Elizabeth: Do you know each other?
>   This is Alice Liam, Sally:
>   You know Alice, Sally, don't you?
>   Sally Keogh, Harry Keogh . . .
>   Oliver, do you know the Halseys?
>   This is Oliver Oren, Helen.
>   Mr and Mrs Keogh, Oliver.
>   (*This Music Crept by Me on
>   the Waters*, 1953)

This is an extreme example of the difficulty of balancing poetry and domestic naturalism. Admittedly Macleish was later able to make the family in *J.B.* (1957) converse fairly naturally in a loose form of poetry, but even so a policeman, announcing the daughter's death, goes to the other extreme when he comments:

> Death is a bone that stammers . . . a tooth
> Among the flints that has forgotten.

The result of this difficulty was that the poetry became pushed more and more into the mouths of a separate chorus. The plays of Auden and Isherwood are almost entirely in sandwich form, with slices of removable poetry between the prose scenes. The best poetry in *The Dog beneath the Skin* (1935) survives as a separate and well-known poem:

> Happy the Hare at morning, for she cannot read
> The Hunter's waking thoughts.

In Eliot's third play, *The Cocktail Party* (1949), there is little recognizable poetry except when four of the house-guests turn themselves, with some embarrassment, into a chorus of Guardians. The poets, having thrown off Shakespeare's influence, found themselves left with a version of the Greek chorus as the only outlet for the lyrical poetry which they wanted to write.

Spender, Auden and Isherwood soon gave up the theatre. Macleish found that the radio was a more feasible medium for this type of poetic drama and wrote two good poetic plays in *The Fall of a City* (1937) and *Air Raid* (1938). (There is not such need for real contact between characters who cannot be seen: in his radio play, *The Trial of Lukullus*, 1939, Brecht uses poetry more extensively than in any of his stage plays.) Eliot, more tenacious than the others, had his own solution.

Oddly enough, none of these dramatists had made much use of that most reliable of all the forms of theatre poetry—the dramatic narrative. Playwrights have always felt able to raise their poetry to a level of richer imagery and greater lyricism when a character has been describing a dramatic event—one has only to think of the messengers' speeches in Greek tragedy and in Racine, or of the Nō plays, or, in Shakespeare, of the Chorus's speeches in Henry V and of Gertrude's account of Ophelia's death. Narrative passages might have been a better vehicle for these dramatists' poetry than the more reflective choruses which they chose to write. They certainly proved very effective in the hands of Brecht and Lorca. Brecht adopted much of the Nō technique in *The Caucasian Chalk Circle* (1945), where a story-teller narrates at the side of the stage while the heroine performs a dumb-show. So, while Grusha sits and washes linen in a stream, far away from her soldier fiancé, the narrator says:

> As she sat by the stream to wash the linen
> She saw his image in the water,
> And his face grew dimmer with the passing moons.
> As she raised herself to wring the linen
> She heard his voice from the murmuring maple
> And his voice grew fainter with the passing moons.
> Evasions and sighs grew more numerous,
> Tears and sweat flowed.
> With the passing moons the child grew up.[14]

Even more effectively, at the end of Lorca's *Blood Wedding* (1933) the Mother tells the neighbours of the disaster which has happened in the play:

C

Neighbours; with a knife,
with a little knife,
on their appointed day, between two and three,
these two men killed each other for love.
With a knife,
with a tiny knife
that barely fits the hand,
but that slides in clean
through the astonished flesh
and stops at the place
where trembles, enmeshed
the dark root of a scream.[15]

By no means all the poetry in *Blood Wedding* is as successful as
this. Much of it sits very uneasily in the play. Lorca had the same
problem as Eliot. They were both primarily poets, attracted by
the theatre above all as an extension of poetry. How were they
to blend their poetry into their plays and create a satisfactory
poetic drama? How avoid mere decoration of drama with
poetry? And how make a modern audience accept the result?
Their solutions are worth comparing.

Eliot had found the perfect subject-matter in *Murder in the
Cathedral*, but he himself called it a 'dead-end'.[16] Even leaving
technical considerations aside, its appeal was too limited. The
theatre is one of the sides of the market place, and that was
where Eliot wanted to be. His solution was to make his later
plays *seem* like ordinary drawing-room comedies, by using
conventional plots and settings and by doing away with his
provocative rhythms in favour of an informal and conversational four-stress line. He was in fact trying to smuggle his
echoes of Greek tragedy and of Christian redemption into the
drawing-room—in the hope that anything will be acceptable
there. But he went too far. In his determination to get the swine
to accept his pearls he ended by hiding them almost entirely in
the swill. His plays have come to seem almost identical with
routine domestic comedies and they have had the appropriate
box-office success. The critic has had to delve deeper and deeper
below the surface of cocktail-party trivialities to find the

authentic Eliot meanings—they are always there somewhere, but the pill has been too well coated with sugar. Auden and Spender left the theatre behind them. Eliot persisted, but at the price of leaving dramatic poetry behind him.

Before comparing Lorca, it is worth mentioning Christopher Fry. He went in a diametrically opposite direction from both Eliot and Lorca. Instead of concealing the poetry, he made it the very *raison d'être* of his art. His comedies play with poetry in the virtuoso way in which Oscar Wilde's played with epigram. So Fry will build up a whole speech round one metaphor, larding it with excellent puns and conceits, or make a character speak a sentence of forty-four lines in one breath. It is all a sophisticated form of exhibitionism, delightful while it lasts, but it inevitably burns itself out quickly. Like Eliot, Fry was at one time thought to be ushering in a new age of poetic drama. For opposite reasons neither of them have been able to do so.

Like *Murder in the Cathedral* Lorca's first full-length play, *Blood Wedding*, provided easy opportunities for poetry, because it was about wild and passionate peasants. Even so, much of the poetry remains intolerably separate from the play. There is a long scene of Claudelian poeticism, in which Death and the Moon speak lengthy speeches, and much of the dialogue is consistent only with its own poetic imagery, rather than with the characters or the situation. So the Mother can say:

> Your father, he used to take me. That's the way with men of good stock; good blood. Your grandfather left a son on every corner. That's what I like. Men, men; wheat, wheat.[17]

This imagery, flatly juxtaposing 'men' and 'wheat', is as artificial as the Mother's final narrative speech, which I quoted above, was natural.

Lorca had gone a long way towards eliminating poeticism in his next play, *Yerma* (1934) (his brother tells how he was displeased by the success of the one scene in it which he considered too lyrical), but his own superb form of poetic drama was not achieved until his third full-length play, *The House of Bernarda Alba* (1936). This contains no actual poetry—by which I mean stressed lines, printed so on the page—but the prose heightens into its own dramatic poetry at the right moments. So the young heroine, in her attempt to get free of her mother, can burst out with:

> I can't stand this horrible house after the taste of his mouth. I'll be what he wants me to be. Everybody in the village against me, burning me with fiery fingers, pursued by those who claim they're decent, and I'll wear, before them all, the crown of thorns that belongs to the mistress of a married man.[18]

This is genuinely the language of poetic drama, and the play is also poetic in another sense—that of the whole play as a poem. Lorca has built it up as a criss-cross fabric of images and symbols, in the way that a poet may build up a poem. The setting itself provides a complete image for this study of maternal dominance—the whole action takes place inside the house of Bernarda Alba, which her five daughters are fighting to get out of.

This form of poetic drama, which has in some respects been continued by Tennessee Williams, is what Arthur Miller had in mind when he wrote, in the Preface to his own plays: 'The underlying poem of a play I take to be the organic necessity of its parts.' Soon after writing *The House of Bernarda Alba* Lorca was killed, at the age of thirty-eight, by the Fascists. Had he lived he might never again have written a line of verse in a play, but he would have become the greatest poetic dramatist of the age.

This leads to the surprising conclusion that the real poetic drama of this century is in prose. Leaving aside the imagistic aspect of poetry, by which a whole play can be a symbolist poem, and concentrating on its rhythmic aspect, there are two main ways in which prose can be patterned and heightened until it achieves the effect of poetry. The first is inside a speech—and the second is from speech to speech, in the ripple of dialogue.

It was perhaps the Abbey Theatre dramatists who first patterned each speech of prose into something near to poetry. With Lady Gregory the medium was still an endlessly repeated balanced line, as dull as the breathing of an artificial lung. For example, from *The Goal Gate* (1906):

> Mary Cushin: What is the man after saying? Sure it cannot be Dennis is dead?
> Gatekeeper: Dead since the dawn of yesterday, and another man now in his cell. I'll go see who has charge of his clothing, if you're wanting to bring it away.
> Mary Cahel: There is lasting kindness in heaven, when no kindness is found upon earth. There will surely be mercy found for him, and not the hard judgement of men.

Synge got free from this strictly rhythmical prose and developed an idiom in which each speech explodes with its own chaos of colours and then always, like a good firework, has one extra and unexpected shower of sparks at the end. Christy Mahon says, characteristically, in *The Playboy of the Western World* (1907):

> It's well you know it's a lonesome thing to be passing small towns with the lights shining sideways when the night is down, or going in strange places with a dog noising before you and a dog noising behind, or drawn to the cities where you'd hear a voice kissing and talking deep love in every shadow of the ditch, and you passing on with an empty, hungry stomach failing from your heart.

This profusion is not to everyone's taste (Kenneth Tynan once described the typical Synge sentence as having 'a trailing tin-can of verbiage' pinned to its tail[19]), but Synge could also use his idiom with impressive simplicity. At the end of *Deirdre of the Sorrows* (1909) the old nurse says:

> Deirdre is dead, and Naisi is dead; and if the oaks and stars could die for sorrow, it's a dark sky and a hard and naked earth we'd have this night in Emain.

This heightened prose was taken over from Synge, together with the mantle of chief Abbey Theatre playwright, by Sean

O'Casey, who wrote his three rich farces (*Juno and the Paycock, The Shadow of a Gunman* and *The Plough and the Stars*) during the twenties. It reappears in the work of various American playwrights, such as Paul Green (in *The House of Connelly*, 1931) and John Howard Lawson (in *Marching Song*, 1937)—usually in the mouths of negro characters, for whom rich language is almost as natural as it is to the Irish—and it continues to crop up here and there, as in John Arden's *Live like Pigs* (1958) and *Sergeant Musgrave's Dance* (1960).

It is, however, the second type of prose poetry which is more prominent in twentieth-century plays and which looks like developing much further—*viz.*, the staccato effect of dialogue made up of short balanced remarks, a sort of jazzed-up stychomythia.

The expressionist satirists, such as Kaiser, Toller and Čapek, had discovered the use of this method. In Čapek's *Insect Play* the two Ant Engineers are explaining to the Tramp why it is necessary that they should wipe out all the other races of ants. They say that it is essential for the 'interests of the whole' and then enlarge:

> 2nd Engineer: The interests of the whole are the highest . . .
> Chief Engineer: Interests of race—
> 2nd Engineer: Industrial interests—
> Chief Engineer: Colonial interests—
> 2nd Engineer: World interests—
> Chief Engineer: Interests of the world—
> 2nd Engineer: Yes, yes, that's it.
> Chief Engineer: All interests are the whole's.
> 2nd Engineer: Nobody may have interests but the whole.
> Chief Engineer: Interests preserve the whole.
> 2nd Engineer: And wars nourish it.[20]

This is a long way from any sort of poetry, but it is right and effective in its own very limited dramatic situation—particularly in the way the last line brings the sequence down to its close with a pat and self-satisfied form of Q.E.D.

This type of dramatic dialogue is usually a duet—two voices can set the rhythm going and then round it off, three or more are likely to blur it. Cocteau used it brilliantly in his *The Bridal Pair of the Eiffel Tower* (1921), in which two gramophones narrate the crazy events and speak all the characters' remarks, while dancers mime the action. Eliot had experimented with it in his dramatic fragment, *Sweeney Agonistes* (1927). But it was brought to its highest peak—and in this case it really can be said to be poetry—by Samuel Beckett in the mouths of his two tramps in *Waiting for Godot* (1952). These two, whose long wait is constantly threatened by boredom, aptly and proudly describe one of their longest runs of repartee as 'not a bad little canter'. The rhythms of the canter are obvious on almost any page of the script. At one point the forgetful Estragon is trying to get straight in his mind the situation with respect to Godot:

Estragon: What exactly did we ask him to do for us?
Vladimir: Were you not there?
Estragon: I can't have been listening
Vladimir: Oh . . . nothing very definite.
Estragon: A kind of prayer.
Vladimir: Precisely.
Estragon: A vague supplication.
Vladimir: Exactly.
Estragon: And what did he reply?
Vladimir: That he'd see.
Estragon: That he couldn't promise anything.
Vladimir: That he'd have to think it over.
Estragon: In the quiet of his home.
Vladimir: Consult his family.
Estragon: His friends.
Vladimir: His agents.
Estragon: His correspondents.
Vladimir: His books.
Estragon: His bank account.
Vladimir: Before taking a decision.
Estragon: It's the normal thing.
Vladimir: Is it not?
Estragon: I think it is.
Vladimir: I think so too. (*silence*)

This dialogue has much of the old music-hall routine of a running patter *à deux*, full of repetition and paraphrase. So also has the discussion about a brass-hat in O'Casey's *The Silver Tassie* (1928):

> 2nd Stretcher Bearer: Does 'e eat well?
> The rest (*in chorus*): Yes, 'e eats well!
> 2nd Stretcher Bearer: Does 'e sleep well?
> The rest: Yes, 'e sleeps well!
> 2nd Stretcher Bearer: Does 'e whore well?
> The rest: Yes, 'e whores well.
> 2nd Stretcher Bearer: Does 'e fight well?
> The rest: Napoo; 'e 'as to do the thinking for the
>   Tommies!

Dramatists as different as Eliot, Dos Passos and Brecht have believed that new life should come into the serious theatre from music-hall and cabaret, and the influence of these arts still continues strongly. The dying music-hall provided John Osborne with both a framework and a symbol for a play about the decay of England (*The Entertainer*, 1957), and ever since his *Look Back in Anger* (1956) it has been almost imperative for the characters in new British left-wing plays to break into spontaneous song-and-dance routines, and for the plays themselves to be larded with little songs.

My examples of this second type of prose-poetry have come from very stylized plays, a long way from any form of naturalism. But the same types of rhythm can be used inside naturalism. Real conversation does contain remarkable patterns of repetition and inversion, and a subtle dramatist can capture and heighten these without losing any sense of reality. A good example is this sequence in Arthur Miller's *A View from the Bridge* (1955). Beatrice and her husband Eddie have been quarrelling about the two Italian immigrants whom she intends to put up. He tells her to stop worrying:

> Beatrice, *looking into his eyes*: I'm just worried about you, that's all I'm worried.

Eddie: Listen, as long as they know where they're gonna sleep.

Beatrice: I told them in the letters. They're sleepin' on the floor.

Eddie: Beatrice, all I'm worried about is you got such a heart that I'll end up on the floor with you, and they'll be in our bed.

Beatrice: All right, stop it.

Eddie: Because as soon as you see a tired relative, I end up on the floor.

Beatrice: When did you end up on the floor?

Eddie: When your father's house burned down I didn't end up on the floor?

Beatrice: Well, their house burned down!

This achieves its effect simply by the repetition of 'worried', 'end up on the floor' and 'burned down'. A similar poetry of naturalism had been attempted by Eliot in parts of *The Waste Land* and in *Sweeney Agonistes*, used by Clifford Odets in *Awake and Sing* and *Golden Boy* in the thirties, and even, as early as 1916, anticipated by Kaiser in one family scene in the otherwise expressionistic *From Morn till Midnight*. But the style is only now coming into its own. It is the main talent of Harold Pinter, who uses Cockney and Jewish dialects as his raw material where Miller uses Brooklyn. To most people the twists and turns and pauses of ordinary conversation merely constitute a chaos which has little to do with art. The conversation overheard on top of a bus has about as much relation to dramatic dialogue as doodling on a piano has to a sonata. But Harold Pinter plunges in and pins down all the repetitions and the crazy extra phrases. So a character in *The Caretaker* asks: 'What's that then, exactly, then?' and a typical speech runs:

I got a mate at Shepherd's Bush, you see . . . I got this mate at Shepherd's Bush. In the convenience. Well, he was in the convenience. Run about the best convenience they had. Run about the best one. Always slipped me a bit of soap, any time I went in there. Very good soap. They have to have the best soap. I was never without a piece of soap, whenever I happened to be knocking about the Shepherd's Bush area.

The effect in the theatre of Pinter's conversational music can be judged by the great success of a revue sketch of his, *Last to Go*, which consisted merely of an aimless chat between an old newspaper-seller and the attendant at a tea-bar. The whole sketch could be analysed in terms of music, with themes re-entering and inverting. A sample passage went:

Old Man: You was a bit busy earlier.
Barman: Ah.
Old Man: Round about ten.
Barman: Ten, was it?
Old Man: About then.
           (*pause*)
    I passed by here about then.
Barman: Oh yes?
Old Man: I noticed you were doing a bit of trade.
           (*pause*)
Barman: Yes, trade was very brisk here about ten.
Old Man: Yes, I noticed.
           (*pause*)
    I sold my last one about then. Yes. About nine forty-five.
Barman: Sold your last one then, did you?
Old Man: Yes, my last *Evening News* it was. Went about twenty to ten.

The revue audience sat entranced. How far the range of this type of dialogue can be extended remains to be seen. Meanwhile a new form of dramatic poetry has been developed—one that is, I suspect, more real and more adaptable than any of the other attempts of this century.

6

The Use of Symbols

SYMBOLS are older than words in drama, which has its roots in primitive rites, enacting in terms of mime and symbol the annual cycle of birth, death and rebirth or the pattern of a hunt. But by the time drama emerges as literature—with Aeschylus—symbols are playing a relatively minor rôle. The characters still have the vestiges of symbolic functions which scholars are able to trace back to their roots, but the only real symbol in the *Agamemnon*, in the sense that we now think of symbols, is the purple carpet which Clytaemnestra lays down for her husband, tempting him towards the *hubris* of walking on it.

That famous carpet will serve to define what I shall mean by symbol in this chapter. The carpet by itself has no meaning. It acquires a meaning only in relation to Agamemnon's actions. Either he will walk on it or he will not—he will commit *hubris* or he will resist the temptation. This, then, is one kind of dramatic symbol, an object that can be used in an action. The only other kind is itself an action—such as Celia's going off to be a missionary in Eliot's *The Cocktail Party*. A symbolic action like this can be planned, discussed, voted for or against and finally acted upon or not acted upon. Her attitude towards it will reveal the degree of her self-fulfilment or of her self-betrayal. Like the carpet, it derives its meaning from the events which surround it. It is a little, but only a little, too sweeping to say that no dramatic symbols have *any* meaning until they are involved in an action. A maypole, for example, can, by itself, be said to be a phallic symbol. But this is only a very limited representational meaning, comparable to the meaning of the word 'tree' taken by itself. The maypole achieves a real symbolic meaning only when men set it up, or dance round it or chop it down.

The action which makes use of symbols is an allegory, and it is allegories which have complete meanings, not symbols. To complete the analogy of words, the individual word 'tree' is a symbol: the sentence, which makes use of words, is an allegory: and it is only when used in sentences that words achieve a full meaning, like symbols in an action. The one essential qualification of a symbol is that it should be capable of being *used*.

This definition rules out much in the theatre that many people refer to as 'symbol'. I prefer to draw the line here between symbols and images. Symbols can be used in an action, images can not—symbols are organic, images descriptive. To give one clear example, the doll's house, the title of Ibsen's play, is an image; it reflects the meaning of the play but cannot be used in the action. On the other hand the wild duck, in the play of that name, is an actual animal in the story which can be loved or hated, fed or killed. It is a symbol.

One of the types of symbol of which the theatre has exclusive use is the concrete or visual symbol. Homer could have written about Agamemnon's carpet but only Aeschylus could show it. Medieval poets did describe exactly this type of symbol —the lover, for example, trying to pluck the rose which represents his lady and being kept off by the thorns of her modesty or disdain—but dramatists, with a very proper fear of bathos, avoided the idiom and continued to avoid it until the last hundred years. Incidents like Richard II's handing over his crown and then snatching it back again are no more typical of Shakespeare than the purple carpet was of Aeschylus.

The movement which prepared the way for modern theatrical symbolism was Naturalism. The determination of Zola and his followers in the second half of the nineteenth century to give the stage-setting the complete appearance of reality brought into being that modern maestro, the props-man. Suddenly furniture, tea-cups, waste-paper baskets, lamps and stoves flooded on to the stage—all the bric-à-brac of real life, and every piece of it a potential symbol. Paradoxical though it may sound, Zola had thrown open the gates for Ionesco.

Ibsen took over the naturalistic stage-setting but put it to a far from naturalistic use. The carefully contrived web of his dialogue was very different from normal drawing-room conversation and, more important to this chapter, the drawing-room furniture was no random selection. In *Ibsen's Dramatic Method* John Northam has extracted from Ibsen's dialogue and stage directions the precise rôle of every lamp, window or alcove. He shows that no light is ever switched on and no curtain ever drawn without Ibsen using the action as a symbolic accompaniment to the dramatic situation. These subtleties are frequently neglected by directors and their point would almost certainly be missed by audiences. But Ibsen also uses much broader symbols, which fit perfectly into the naturalistic framework, even though nobody could fail to notice their symbolic status. So Hedvig's wild duck is clearly more than a wild duck and Hedda Gabbler's burning of Eilert's manuscript is nearer to child-murder than to literary vandalism. Ibsen is often called the father of modern drama. This claim may be too sweeping, but he is indisputably the father of modern dramatic symbolism.

Some use of symbol since Ibsen has been superb. A good example is the last scene of O'Neill's *Long Day's Journey into Night.* The mother, a pathetic drug-addict, drifts in, dragging behind her the wedding dress which she has just dug out of a trunk. She is remembering her young days and this limp off-white object symbolizes perfectly her memories. Then her husband takes it from her and holds it in his arms 'with an unconscious, clumsy, protective gentleness'. In his arms it becomes something nearer to herself, the beautiful young wife whom he married long ago and who has turned so tragically into this creature. In a long final speech she gropes her way clumsily through her memories in O'Neill's peculiarly drab language. The whole effect is extremely moving and says much more than words alone could—unless they were Shakespeare's. But in lesser hands symbols can merely weigh banality down to its very depths. In Inge's *Come Back Little Sheba* the middle-aged couple's lost youth is symbolized by a small lost dog (Sheba), which the wife keeps calling for outside the door; and at the end of the play this woman's new state of unselfishness is neatly symbolized by a rare and exciting occurrence—she cooks breakfast for her husband.

An analysis of the different uses of visual symbolism in the

theatre could be endless. It can extend from the whole stage-
setting down to tiny isolated incidents—from the bedroom in
O'Neill's *All God's Chillun Got Wings*, which shrinks as the couple
get more and more on each other's nerves, down to Blanche
Dubois' insistence on covering the bare light-bulbs with
delicate shades in *A Streetcar Named Desire*. We have by now come
to accept this visual symbolism as a normal dramatic idiom.
But, to remind oneself how comparatively new it is, one has only
to try to imagine a symbolic prop like Laura's collection of
glass animals (in Tennessee Williams' *The Glass Menagerie*) on any
stage earlier than Ibsen's.

In none of my examples has the symbol or the symbolic
event been the backbone of the whole play, or even of a whole
scene. It has been something nearer to an embellishment—an
extra detail which is, however, in no sense irrelevant, since it
reflects the central theme and strengthens an audience's
impression of it. But the last scene of *Long Day's Journey into
Night* would still make perfect sense without the wedding
dress.

Recently, however, a form of symbolic drama has grown up
which gives the symbols a much more central place—allows
them, in fact, to shape the whole form of the play. Eugène
Ionesco, the leading practitioner of this school, perversely likes
to call his theatre 'anti-theatre'. It is a misleading name, since
his style could more relevantly be called 'theatricalism'. He has
taken to their extreme the elements of the theatre which are
peculiar to it. His better plays rely so fully on props and on
visual effects that most of their impact is inevitably lost on the
printed page.

His *Amédée, or How to Get Rid of It* is about a married couple
who have a sizable problem in their flat. The corpse of a man,
which has been there for fifteen years, is steadily growing and
threatens to crowd them out entirely. Meanwhile mushrooms
sprout from the floor, the walls and the ceiling. In their shame
and fear Amédée and his wife have shut themselves off from
the rest of the world. The play shows their reactions to this
corpse, their quarrels over it, their dusting of it and their
attempts to get rid of it. It and the mushrooms are the only

two symbols of decay in the play. They are treated completely
naturalistically by the couple—i.e. simply as a very large corpse,
by now well over twenty feet long, and an annoying plague of
mushrooms—and by virtue of this they need never be tied down
to one interpretation. When the symbolism was only partial or
incidental it could be specifically interpreted. Blanche Dubois'
covering of the naked bulbs can represent only her inability to
face ugly reality. But this corpse can be taken to mean anything
from a crime in the past to, say, a nagging worry about bad
breath. It could even be a real corpse. It can be anything, in fact,
which could be at the root of an obsession, because the small
details—their constant desire to take a peep at the corpse, for
example, and their shame at doing so—will hold true in every
instance. So Ionesco is able to present symbolically a complete
and detailed drama of an obsession, without having to limit it
to any specific case. In his *The New Tenant* a man moves into an
empty flat and is soon swamped by his possessions—bits of
furniture, vases, pictures and general bric-à-brac. He treats all
these objects quite straightforwardly; as, with less affection,
do the bewildered furniture-removers. The objects come to
represent what each member of the audience wills; happy
memories of the past, protective inhibitions, real souvenirs,
anything. Many human experiences follow the same subjective
patterns, regardless of the details, and Ionesco finds a symbol
that will be theatrically effective, however fantastic, and with it
provides a blue-print of one such pattern. In the case of *The
New Tenant*, with the entire stage piled up to the roof with
furniture and the hero hidden amongst it, one does seem to
have reached the end of a long line from Zola.

Less complete than Ionesco, but using something of the same
technique, is Jean Genet. His particular version of visual
symbolism is in dressing up. In *The Maids* two domestic servants
go through a very elaborate charade of dressing each other up
as their half-hated, half-admired mistress. The exact psychology
of their attitude to the mistress, with all its opposing com-
plexities, is superbly brought out by Genet in the symbolic
terms of this charade. In the same way a plumber in his play *The
Balcony* is dressed up by a prostitute to become a great general.

The contrast between the two (both ridiculous) reflects constantly on each. The general is an eight-foot-tall figure who clops about in raised boots. He would be farcical enough even if we had not seen the timid little man he was made of.

Clothes are used in a similar way by Brecht in a scene in *Galileo*. The pope wants to leave Galileo unmolested. A cardinal visits the pope while he is being dressed and argues that the Holy Church needs Galileo to be silenced. As the huge robes are piled on the pope, the man disappears inside the office. By the end of the scene all that is left of him is a tiny face in the middle of all the magnificence—and he is powerless to disagree with the cardinal.

I am not suggesting that this type of full-scale symbolism is a new 'discovery' of the last few years—merely that it has been more widely used recently. There are examples of it as long ago as the days of Strindberg and Maeterlinck, and it was put to excellent use in the Living Newspapers, part of the Federal Theatre Project in the late thirties.

A scene in *One Third of a Nation*, one of the Living Newspapers, depicts the creation of a slum by a speculator's ruthless exploitation of his property. His piece of land is represented by a grass mat, which he unrolls on the stage. He sits tenants down on this mat, where they start to perform the routine of living—washing, shaving, eating, sleeping, kissing. As more and more people arrive, the speculator raises his price, steadily at first and then, as space becomes very limited, more sharply. Eventually the mat is completely full. The speculator's profit has been vast and he is about to leave, to repeat his killing elsewhere, when an enormously fat man appears and asks for accommodation. The speculator at first refuses, but is soon unable to resist the sum offered. With a great shove he sends the fat man hurtling into the seething mass of humanity. The lights go out.

This, like the scenes from Ionesco, Genet and Brecht, is entirely successful, but there are dangers in the method. In *Endgame* Samuel Beckett presents the relationship of an old couple in a purely symbolic form. They each live in a dustbin. Occasionally they pop their heads up for air, or to continue the old man's interminable story. Then they want to kiss: they lean over towards each other: their lips cannot quite reach: the dustbins are too far apart. Surprisingly, this is successful in the theatre, but it comes dangerously close to the banal, and Beckett does, in fact, sink to the purely banal when he follows this type of visual symbolism to its logical conclusion in *Acts without Words*, a dumb-show which was devised as a companion piece to *Endgame*. In it a tramp sits silently on the stage. A branch grows from a tree. He moves under it for the shade and it promptly withers. A carafe of water comes down on a string. Whenever he makes a grab at it it is jerked up out of his reach; and when it does finally stay down he is too tired, or bored, to lift a hand to it. This may be a tenable view of human life—but the symbols have become so general that they are merely obvious.

7

In Search of Significance

THANKS to anthropology, sociology, psychology and all the other new methods of analysis, the world has become self-conscious. The playwrights of the last eighty years, finding deep significance in the drama of other ages, have had to feel certain that their work provides the same. Unfortunately the new self-consciousness came at a time when the straight line of theatrical tradition had collapsed.

If Shakespeare or Aeschylus had had modern analysis explained to them they would not in any way have had to alter their methods of playwriting. They would have found, probably much to their surprise, that their works stood the test as they were. I am not, of course, suggesting that these dramatists were quite unaware of what they were doing— merely that their approach to their work was different. The 'rôle of theatre in society' has never been better exemplified than in Athens, but there is no mention of it in Aristotle's *Poetics*. In contrast to these, if the plays of Scribe and Sardou had been subjected to modern analysis they would have been puffed right away—as, indeed, they now have been. The first half of the nineteenth century was the hey-day of romantic poetry, but it was a low ebb for the drama. All possible 'significance' had drained away from the theatre. For anyone coming after Scribe and Sardou, from Zola and Ibsen onwards, it was a question of laboriously building significance in again. And this is lonely and self-conscious work.

When Shakespeare wrote 'The world's a stage' he was making a point about the world. When Arnold Wesker has a character in *The Kitchen* saying that the world is like a kitchen he is instead making a point about his own play—he is emphasizing, in case we should have missed it, his play's general significance, its relevance for the whole of human life.

Similarly, O'Neill introduces each of the plays in his trilogy, *Mourning becomes Electra*, with a crowd scene—to give the play its setting in society, he explains—and for the same purpose Arthur Miller stipulates that the Lomans' house in *Death of a Salesman* shall be merely the transparent frame of a house, so that 'we see a solid vault of apartment houses around the small, fragile-seeming home'.

This desire for social significance would, one might suspect, lead to a naturalistic style of playwriting—'real' people in 'real' situations. But there are several snags to naturalistic situations in the theatre. One is that they tend to seem too particular, to lack relevance for the rest of the world outside this situation. Another is that they are always liable to be interrupted by the police or the telephone or some other safeguard of modern life—characters in a naturalistic play have none of the anarchic freedom to act out their passions that Shakespeare's or Racine's kings and queens enjoyed. Or again, if a play takes place in a setting which is familiar in real life, such as a sitting-room or a workshop, the audience will start judging it by standards of verisimilitude. 'But it just isn't like that', they may object. Thus the playwright will be tied down by the tiny details and how-do-you-do's of everyday life, just as he will have to waste his precious minutes in creating convincing exits and entrances. Finally there is the objection that naturalistic scenes lack grandeur. Almost every age wants its art to have grandeur and the twentieth century has been as eager as any to write high tragedy.

In spite of these difficulties there does remain a feeling that significant plays should be set in the here and now. It was reflected by the *Observer's* ruling, in its play competition in 1957, that all entries must be set in the previous ten years. This mistaken concept of how a play may best be 'contemporary' is perhaps merely a lurking reaction against those heavy and romantic slices of historical life so much favoured by the Victorians: but the successor of these is the Hollywood epic, not the Brechtian. Whatever its reason, this desire to use contemporary and near-naturalistic settings while remaining free of their limitations has led to various solutions. Eliot and O'Neill, in pursuit of grandeur, concealed echoes of Greek tragedy in their modern drawing-rooms. Ugo Betti, dramatizing in *The Burnt Flower Bed* a struggle of ends versus means and of politics versus people, chose modern politicians as his characters and then found convincing reasons for bringing them together in a mountain cottage, with the telephone lines cut and escape or rescue made impossible. His drama was then free to develop without interruption—and, more important, without the audience asking *why* there was no interruption. Charles Morgan had tried something similar in *The Flashing Stream* and *The Burning Glass*, but with less success. Like Betti's, his themes are timeless moral problems which could be set in any place or period. He chose, presumably in order to emphasize their contemporary importance, to give them a modern political setting. Unfortunately, where Betti's symbols and situations are watertight, Morgan's are not. We are asked to believe in *The Burning Glass* that one man could alone have found a formula that would destroy the world, and in *The Flashing Stream* that the government and electorate of Great Britain see science as a mere series of sums. In both plays the moral dilemma and the struggle with the authorities could be very real indeed, but they are each time invalidated by the loop-holes in their shaky modern setting. It just would not happen like that, we are once more left free to protest. Ironically enough, the subject-matter of *The Flashing Stream* has been presented much more effectively by Hochwälder in *The Strong are Lonely* and by Brecht in *Galileo*—the first being set in the eighteenth century and the second in the seventeenth.

The fact is that 'significance' is much more easily achieved with a little distancing—one can see the truth of a home-truth rather better away from home. We tend to think of Shakespeare's plays as being essentially of his time. So they are in spirit, but not in subject-matter; none of the tragedies or problem-plays are set in sixteenth-century England. In the same way, although the plays of Aeschylus reflect closely the attitudes of early fifth-century Athens and those of Euripides late fifth-century Athens, both dramatists used, almost exclusively, mythological subject-matter. And Racine explained at length that he felt justified in writing a modern tragedy, *Bajazet*, only because it was set in a land as far away as Turkey. The here and the now have always been the habitat of comedy—against Euripides, Shakespeare and Racine set Aristophanes, Ben Jonson and Molière. When dramatists did finally succeed in treating contemporary situations seriously, the particular trappings of the situation frequently overwhelmed their wider meaning. Ibsen's plays, with a few exceptions, are about the spiritual life of the individual and about love. They have been accepted by the world as 'problem' plays—i.e. as very specific. To this extent his naturalistic settings swamped him.

It is significant that Brecht, who would come to most people's lips as the modern theatre's foremost pedlar of contemporary messages, gave all his greatest plays a setting far removed in time or place from his audience—*The Caucasian Chalk Circle* and *The Good Woman of Setzuan* in the East, *Mother Courage* and *Galileo* in past centuries. More than any other modern dramatist Brecht has understood the relationship between general significance and the contemporary scene. When he wanted to make a comment on a specific situation in one place and moment in history, he gave up all pretence of weaving his detailed significance into a story. Instead he wrote, in *Fear and Misery in the Third Reich*, a panorama of life in Nazi Germany in twenty-eight disconnected scenes. By not trying to merge the two elements —of general and of particular significance—he avoided the artificiality of Rice's *We, the People* or of Priestley's *The Linden Tree*. Elmer Rice's attempt to weave all his different protests about the contemporary scene into one coherent story was dazzling, but inevitably also, in all the contortions and coincidences, on the verge of the laughable. *The Linden Tree* was a little more subtle. Priestley limited his range of characters to one family, but the different attitudes inside the family still seem much too obviously chosen as representative of post-war England. The play is killed by the tug-of-war between its two elements—the story and the social survey. Robert Bolt's *The Tiger and the Horse*, which tries to do the same thing for the England of the late fifties and happens, also, to be set in a professor's family, has the same weaknesses.

The expressionists had tried to achieve an air of wide significance by keeping their characters and their situations entirely general. So The Man, The Worker and Adam stomped the boards and the world was their setting. But the results were not so much general as inhuman and no inhuman play can be significant—except, of course, in its failure. One solution adopted by many modern dramatists has been to make a compromise between the very general and the very particular by setting their plays in villages and small towns. These, for the sake of the play, can be regarded as sealed-off units. All authority can reside in the Mayor, just as the Priest can comfortably represent the whole Church, and inside the town walls life can go on as richly and as symbolically as the playwright wishes. He has under his control the whole of humanity on a manageable and familiar scale. The freedom which Brecht found in a Chinese setting, such dramatists as Camus (*The Siege*), Dürrenmatt (*The Visit*), Macleish (*The Fall of a City*) and John Arden (*Sergeant Musgrave's Dance*) found in a small town.

T. S. Eliot and Samuel Beckett provide an interesting comparison in this respect. Both are dealing with themes of the widest significance, nothing less than the relationship of man to man and of man to God. Yet neither wants to appear pompous and remote in the way that Milton, who expressed similar intentions, might be said to be. They desire their drama to be on a grand scale without seeming out of touch with the modern world. They intend it—to express the reverse of the same coin— to be topical without being trivial. Obviously if a modern tycoon or journalist is going to talk in cosmic or high tragic terms the result can be only ludicrous and bathetic. Eliot's solution has been to debase the terms, hoping that the dialogue of his bourgeois characters will sound, on the surface, convincing and acceptable, even though it is, in fact, an artificially contrived web of Christian and mythological allusions. The effect of grandeur is to be achieved almost subliminally. Beckett's solution has been the opposite. He has debased his characters until they become tramps and sink through the bottom of the class structure to a level where no one will think of applying the naturalistic criterion of probability. Tramps are the lowest common

denominator of humanity and everyone, paradoxically, is
prepared to see their own image in them. (The romantic idea
of a tramp seems to have survived Orwell's *Down and Out in
London and Paris*.) So Beckett has an easy symbol for the whole
human race, unrestricted by naturalistic requirements, and his
tramps can discuss their problems—waiting for relief, being
beaten, dreading boredom and futility, as well as the possibility
of Christian redemption and the whole meaning of life—in the
widest of terms without ever seeming pretentious. And any
symbol will be acceptable. Merely getting through a night
without being beaten passes for a sort of happiness. A carrot
instead of the usual turnip can seem a rare delight and one never
questions the two tramps' sense of boredom—by suggesting
that they should go to a film or evening classes, take up raffia-
work or a novel—in the way that some audiences were able to
question Jimmy Porter's frustration in *Look Back in Anger*. ('Why
doesn't he get a more interesting job if he's so intelligent?')

Harold Pinter achieves the same freedom with his tramp in
The Caretaker. The old man's constant plan for going down to
Sidcup to collect his papers comes easily to represent all human
dreams of definite and responsible action. Eliot, being nearer to
naturalism, or at least to the emaciated form of it which takes
place in stage drawing-rooms, is much less free in his choice of
symbols. Each has to justify itself individually against the yard-
stick of the spectator's own life. There are in *The Family Reunion*
two symbols of self-fulfilment through strength. The first,
Harry's departure to be a missionary, is satisfactory: it is far
enough away from the world of everyday reality. But the second
is Mary's dream of becoming a fellow of a women's college.
This is merely bathetic; and oddly enough it is, because of the
context, a less convincing ideal than that of just getting down
to Sidcup.

Other dramatists have found in classical settings a freedom
similar to Beckett's. Again, their method was the opposite of
Eliot's. Where he tried to set classical themes and allusions in
modern contexts, they boldly transplanted modern situations
back into a classical setting. His approach was a restriction, since
his naturalistic surface was exacting and his allusions hard to

accommodate, but the classical settings of Giraudoux, Anouilh, Sartre and others were a freedom from restriction. The difference is that a failure in verisimilitude is distracting whereas anachronisms are usually delightful.

The new classicists made no pretence about period. In the first few lines after her entrance Anouilh's Antigone describes the dawn as having been like a picture postcard. The classical story serves merely as a ready-made framework for a drama of modern dilemmas. The dramatist is freed from the effort of justifying his plot and the whole focus of the play can be on the question in point.

Mythology proved a fund rich enough to meet any requirements. Gide, whose view of life was primarily religious, believed in the submission of man to God; Sartre, mainly a political animal, in man's self-assertion against God. So Gide in his *Oedipus* was able to interpret the Oedipus story as that of a man who was plunged further and further into evil actions simply because he refused to confess, and repent of, the first one. If he had at the time confessed his murder of the old man in the road, Gide argues, he would have discovered that the man was his father and the rest of the horrors would have been avoided. Instead he tried to escape his guilt and took refuge in heroic action, by facing the Sphinx. From his triumph over it the further evils followed inevitably. Sartre was able to draw precisely the opposite moral from the Orestes story. The great virtue of his Orestes in *The Flies* is that he overcomes his sense of guilt and is therefore free to take the murderous action which saves Argos from tyranny. In each of these plays guilt and action are set against each other, but Gide's black is Sartre's white and vice versa: Oedipus's failing was Orestes' virtue. Greek myth provides the ideal blue-print.

Part of the freedom of a mythical setting lies in the audience's knowledge of how the play must end. Orestes must kill Clytaemnestra. Antigone must die. It is this more than anything else which directs the audience's attention away from the plot and on to the playwright's treatment of it—or, in other words, away from the particular and towards the general significance. It also provides many highly dramatic moments. We know, for example, that there can be no compromise for Medea and Jason and it is this knowledge in Anouilh's play which makes Medea's pathetic attempt at reconciliation so poignant. Jason has said that he hopes to find with his new bride 'something which couldn't possibly be more remote from you; happiness, mere happiness'. There is a pause, then:

> Medea: Happiness. *Another pause. Then she suddenly speaks in a small, humble voice, without moving.* Jason, it is hard to say this, almost impossible. The words choke me and make me ashamed. But if I said that I was going to try from now on, with you and me, would you believe me?
> Jason: No.
> Medea, *after a pause*: You would be right. So there we are. With everything said.

This comes at the end of a long meeting between Medea and Jason, in which they look back over their life together in a mixture of sorrow and anger. The traditional plot takes up very little of the play—much less, certainly, than in Euripides' *Medea*. Anouilh uses it merely to float this great final meeting, this moment which fascinates him, because it is out of time and in the very teeth of fate. As soon as it ends Medea will have to carry out her terrible vengeance.

This scene in *Medea* has what the Chorus in Anouilh's *Antigone* means when he says:

> Tragedy is so precise. It is restful, it is certain . . . above all it is calm, because one knows that there is no more hope, no more sordid hope; one knows that one is caught, caught in a trap like a rat . . . Little Antigone is caught. Little Antigone will be able to be her real self for the first time.

It is like the central scene between Creon and Antigone, or the meeting between Hector and Ulysses in *Tiger at the Gates*, both of which are described in Chapter 3. The irony and the force of all these scenes which hang suspended on the brink of inevitability, and indeed the essence of this particular use of well-known classical plots, are expressed in the French title of *Tiger at the Gates*: *La Guerre de Troie n'aura pas Lieu*; The Trojan war will not take place. Even before the curtain goes up we know that it will.

I said earlier that modern dramatists felt the need for their works to have both general significance and grandeur. A classical setting helps towards the former by freeing the dramatist from the particular; but playwrights have also hoped that classical allusions will add grandeur to their plays, on the grounds that Greek theatre is the fountain-head of drama and contains such archetypal dramatic forces as Fate and the Furies. The intention has been, by incorporating details of Greek tragedy, to graft the new drama to powerful roots. But in effect the alien details are likely to remain as extraneous as the Gothic turrets with which the Victorians, for a similar purpose, adorned their buildings.

This is certainly true of the Furies in Eliot's *The Family Reunion*. As the play is written, they are suddenly revealed behind a curtain in this ordinary English country house. Even the stage direction makes plain the awkwardness of the combination: 'The curtains part, revealing the Eumenides in the window embrasure.' This in production can only be ridiculous, and Eliot himself admitted in 1950 that producers would be wise to leave his Eumenides to the audience's imagination.[21] O'Neill devised a slightly more successful version of them in *Mourning becomes Electra*, his adaptation of the *Oresteia*—Orin Mannon, his Orestes, becomes haunted by the old family portraits hanging round the walls. Both Eliot and O'Neill tried to suggest fate in these plays by means of resemblance. Harry Monchensey, the hero of *The Family Reunion*, becomes able to face his own murderous impulses against his wife when he discovers that his father felt similarly towards his mother. O'Neill used the same idea, but in purely physical terms and to excess. The stamp of doom is recognizable on his New England family by the mask-like resemblance which they all, including even the domestic staff, possess. Eliot, always trying to modify the Greek echoes in his drama to make them acceptable, had by the time of his fourth play, *The Confidential Clerk*, turned this idea of resemblance into a case of mere inherited talents. His hero gets the courage to become an organist when he discovers that his father also was one. Unfortunately, once the symbol becomes usual enough to be acceptable, the echo which it embodies is almost too faint to be noticed.

Arthur Miller introduces a note of Fate into *A View from the Bridge* when the lawyer, Alfieri, who is himself a version of the Greek chorus, says how he normally went home at six, but on one December day stayed in his office for no particular reason. He goes on, referring to Eddie Carbone, the hero:

> ... when I saw him walking through my doorway, I knew why I had waited ... Almost transfixed I had come to feel. I had lost my strength somewhere.

This hint of doom may be too tactful to annoy an audience (though it is also doubtful whether it does anything to heighten the play into tragedy), but the same could certainly not be said of Macleish's *Panic*. In this play about the financial crash the ticker-tape machine which clicks out the bad news becomes associated with the Furies, and the spokesman of the workers, who prophesies the financier's doom, is a blind man 'with a white ecstatic face' who has powers of clairvoyance and who strongly, far too strongly, recalls Tiresias.

These examples have been of attempts to magnify modern plays by studding them with relics of the more magnificent Greek drama. They have been attempts to castellate cottages and in this respect they have been failures. There is, however, one play which has brilliantly succeeded in acquiring a classical flavour—O'Neill's *Desire under the Elms*. It is nearer to Racine than to the Greeks, but then Racine took the Greeks as his masters. He used his classics in the way they should be used, he adapted them and made them his own. As a result, his theatre was genuinely neoclassical, with the *neo* carrying as much weight, if not twice as much, as the *classical*. On this basis *Desire under the Elms*, rare among twentieth-century plays, could be called neo-neoclassical.

It is a story of greed on a New England farm in the middle of the last century. The farmer, Old Cabot, married his second wife twenty-five years ago purely in order to get the title-deeds of the farm into his own hands. Their son, Eben, knows this and also believes that his father killed his mother by overworking her. Not surprisingly he hates his father and is determined to get possession of the farm himself as soon as possible. Then Old Cabot marries a third wife, Abbie—partly to spite Eben. Abbie is only a few years older than Eben and now her greed is added to the others'. She makes Old Cabot promise that if she bears him a son he will leave the farm to him entirely, cutting Eben out of his will. She then sets about seducing Eben, hoping to have a son by him and to pass it off as Old Cabot's. At this point the tight mesh of ambition turns to one of passion, because Abbie is also genuinely attracted to Eben. Her scheming ends in a deep and genuine love for him. He feels the same for her and is content to comply in the pretence that his newly born son is really his father's, until one day his father gloatingly tells him of the promise which Abbie made him give. Abbie, in a mad attempt to prove her love for Eben by removing the object of her original plot, now kills her baby. Eben, doubly maddened by this, fetches the sheriff to her and then suddenly, at the last minute, maintains that he killed the child with her. Old Cabot is left alone on his farm as the sheriff takes them off. And the sheriff's last words, looking around as they leave, are: 'It's a jim-dandy farm, no denyin'. Wish I owned it.'

The stark simplicity of this play, both in the writing and in the strict concentration on the theme, raises a plot that could have become melodrama into tragedy. But the play also contains a sense of doom which, without ever seeming extraneous, does help to give it a classical quality. Eben's mother, for example, haunts the play like a figure of ill-omen because of Eben's conviction that his father killed her. So his father's harsh treatment of her looms like a crime in the past, awaiting expiation: she becomes the Thyestes or the King Hamlet of the plot. Fate too is easily suggested by the superstitions of these country people. Old Cabot is convinced for two reasons that it is his destiny to stay on this bleak farm. First, he left it as a young man for richer land out West and yet, when he was already prospering there, something about New England pulled him back to the harder life. And secondly, at the end of the play and after the disaster, when he again plans to leave, he finds that his sons (he also had two by his first wife) have long since taken the horde of money which he had hidden under a floorboard. This is enough to convince him that it is God's will that he should stay where he is and that God sent him evil grasping sons so that His will should be effected. As with the oracle in Greek tragedy, all that matters is that the characters involved believe it. So O'Neill's use of superstitious fatalism becomes a much more effective modern version of Fate than any specific Greek echoes or freaks of physiognomy can be.

One other by-product of using a classical setting is worth mentioning—it is the pleasure of sophistication, the pleasure of getting the point. It is at the root, for example, of Cocteau's *The Infernal Machine*, in which he presents very cynically the events leading up to the point at which Sophocles' play *Oedipus Rex* begins. An audience will miss the entire contrast if it does not already know Sophocles' play. The same is true of Giradoux's reference to Homer in the last line of *Tiger at the Gates*:

The Trojan poet is dead. And now the Grecian poet will have his say.

There is an element of mutual flattery in this between playwright and audience, but then perhaps there is in all sophistication. It is not surprising that the authors of such plays are usually French.

This type of wit is essentially in the spirit of playing with the theatre, because it is incompatible with the complete sense of illusion by which an audience can almost forget that it is in a theatre at all, and the idea of playing with the theatre brings this chapter full circle—back to the lack of tradition, back to the clean slate offered to every new dramatist. With no generally accepted theatrical conventions each new dramatist can make his own conventions and as quickly break them. A modern audience can never be certain what will confront it when it steps into a theatre: a rich tasselled curtain or a set already revealed; a proscenium arch, an apron-stage or an arena; as décor, a realistic room, skeleton houses or just a seat and a bush; Stanislavski actors, Brechtian 'demonstrators' or mere puppet-figures. When such flexibility is the norm, the theatrical conventions become magic tools in a dramatist's hands. He can spring from one to another, he can mix them in new proportions. A great many of his effects will involve playing with the theatre and it can be played with for a variety of purposes, from didacticism to delight. So Brecht makes a chorus break into a hopeless situation in *The Good Woman of Setzuan* to ask the audience whether *they* can think of any possible way out of the calamity that has befallen their heroine; and Giradoux opens *Sodom and Gomorrah* like this:

> The gardener: Well, isn't that the most beautiful curtain-raising that an audience will ever be offered! Up it goes, and what do they see?—the archangel of archangels.
> The archangel: Let them make the best of it quickly. It won't last long. And the spectacle to follow is likely to be terrible.
> The gardener: I know. The prophets are announcing it. The end of the world.

These effects are, respectively, pointful and witty. Inevitably many modern dramatists who juggle with the conventions are neither. An accepted convention in the theatre, such as Shakespeare and his contemporaries inherited, provides a basis for the great dramatist to rise from and a framework in which the ordinary dramatist can write at his best. The great freedom of this century has been a stimulating challenge to the few good playwrights—the ones who take up the remaining part of this book. Its disadvantage is that it has left the less talented ones floundering.

PART THREE

The Dramatists

8

The Choice of Cast

IN CHOOSING which dramatists to treat individually in this part of the book I have been ruled, first of all, by a distinction between 'dramatists' and 'playwrights'. By 'playwright', with its implication of craft rather than art, I mean an author who takes a likely subject and turns it into a play; by 'dramatist' I mean one who develops through his plays a personal vision. Only 'dramatists' are worth serious critical consideration, and this rules out authors such as Terence Rattigan, however competent they may be. It even rules out Elmer Rice.

Beyond this criterion my choice of dramatists was limited by space: if each author is treated too briefly, criticism becomes cataloguing. The maximum number seemed to be eight or nine, and the list became Pirandello, O'Neill, Brecht, Giradoux, Anouilh, Sartre, Eliot, Williams and Miller. Other candidates were Lorca, but his output was small and he has already loomed large in Chapter 5; O'Casey, but he never again reached the standard of his first three plays in the twenties and his later work has grown more and more out of touch with the theatre; Salacrou and Betti, but they are not so well known internationally as they should be and a short chapter is not the place in which to try to establish reputations. By the opposite token, Eliot's reputation demands a chapter for him though his merit might not; since he is widely known and discussed, his absence would seem a glaring gap. The same is true of Sartre.

9

Luigi Pirandello 1867–1936

> The world of international literary criticism has been crowded for a long time with numerous Pirandellos—lame, deformed, all head and no heart, erratic, gruff, insane and obscure—in whom, no matter how hard I try, I cannot recognize myself, not even in the slightest degree.

PIRANDELLO wrote these words in 1935 in his foreword to Vittorini's *The Drama of Luigi Pirandello*, a foreword full of gratitude for a book which refuted the current image of him as an intellectual acrobat, a mere prince of paradox. Yet this attitude is still widely held today, and even those who have felt the great passion in the plays tend to fall back on Pirandello's own statement

> One of the novelties that I have given to the modern drama consists in converting the intellect into passion

as being sufficient to explain his power. But this idea still puts the cart before the horse—it makes the original creative impulse of his work an intellectual impulse. It makes it possible for people to describe *Right You Are, If You Think So!* (1917), which is a searing protest against stripping people of their defensive fantasies, as merely a harsh *jeu d'esprit* about the nature of truth. One gets nearer to a description of Pirandello's theatre if one reverses his maxim and says that he turns passion into intellect. This is what many of his central characters do. Their reaction to the suffering in their lives is, in some cases, to withdraw into an intellectual stronghold where emotion is excluded, in others to invent a logical lie which makes the suffering tolerable. Pirandello had to do something similar in his own life.

His personal life was more than usually relevant to his writing. His marriage was an arranged match with a girl whom he had never met, the daughter of his father's partner in a sulphur-mining business. A few years later two disasters coincided. His wife had great difficulty in giving birth to their third child, and the family business went bankrupt when all the sulphur mines were flooded. The shock of these two events unsettled her mind, and the form that her insanity took was jealousy. To calm her, Pirandello stayed at home the whole time and even gave her all the money he earned, but her hysterical accusations of betrayal became more frequent and more violent. He accepted a physician's advice not to put her into an asylum and withdrew, like many of his characters, into silence, appalled that her totally false image of him was a force in the life of the household more powerful than his real self. So the concern in the plays over questions of illusion and reality came directly from his own experience. It was a concern distilled in agony, not a mere philosophical interest. To add to his troubles, his elder son had been taken prisoner in the war, his younger son was very ill and his daughter had tried to commit suicide. It is not surprising that Pirandello's view of life was black.

Yet his first major play is amazingly sunny. Liola (1916) is a story of a double deceit. Simone, an elderly miser, is married to young Mita. They have no children because, as everyone knows, old Simone is impotent. Meanwhile Tuzza, an ambitious girl who is jealous of Mita, is pregnant by the local Adonis, Liola. She concocts a plan. She tells old Simone the truth, but suggests that he announces the baby to be his, thus proving himself not impotent. The idea delights him and he even changes his will in the baby's favour, but Liola goes one better to help the unfortunate Mita. He and Mita have always been attracted to each other, and how much more delighted old Simone would be, he argues, if it were his wife who was having a baby. So Mita too is soon pregnant, Simone disowns Tuzza's baby and changes his will back; and Liola, a carefree soul and, as such, a very rare bird in Pirandello's plays, strolls happily off.

A few months later Pirandello wrote a play treating a similar subject, but from the opposite point of view—Think It Over, Giacomino (1916). An old schoolmaster, Professor Toti, who is no friend of bureaucracy, conceives a plan for doing someone a good turn at the government's expense. He will marry a young wife and she will then be able to go on drawing his pension for another fifty years. He chooses Lillina—an obvious choice for him, because she is pregnant and he will therefore be helping her in yet another way. His only condition is that she shall go on seeing her lover, Giacomino. The behaviour of this trio scandalizes the neighbours, with their conventional ideas of love and marriage, but Professor Toti, and Pirandello, would consider it scandalous if Lillina stopped seeing Giacomino, or if Toti expected her to make love to an old man like himself.

These two plays form the basic pattern which Pirandello was to use in more agonized versions many times during the next few years. One gets used to the strange logical extensions of accepted social and sexual relationships which his characters invent. The invention is presented by Pirandello as evil when it is made for reasons of gain, like Simone's and Tuzza's, but good and demanding of respect when it has defensive or charitable motives, like Toti's. With strict moral justice the evil inventions almost invariably end in disaster, while the good are rewarded.

The Rules of the Game (1918) and *The Pleasure of Honesty* (1917) follow the pattern of *Liola.* In the former a wife who is estranged from her husband tries to make it seem that she has been indecently approached by a young gallant, known for his brilliance at duelling. She hopes that her husband, Leone, will fulfil his conventional obligations, challenge the young man to a duel, get killed and thus leave her free to enjoy life with her lover. Rather to her surprise, Leone does issue the challenge and chooses her lover as his second, but when the appointed dawn comes they find him still in bed. He says he has no intention of actually fighting the duel. He issued the challenge, a purely nominal function, because he is still his wife's nominal husband. But as her lover is her real husband it is his responsibility to perform the act itself. So her lover does fight the duel (as the second, he has to if the principal fails to turn up) and is killed.

Leone therefore did the same as Liola—carried his opponents' game to its logical conclusion till they were hoist on their own petard; and he revealed, in doing so, the *lack* of logic in conventional behaviour. But, unlike Liola, Leone is not a carefree soul.

He is one of Pirandello's typical heroes, whom great suffering in the past has forced to retire into a shell of intellectual detachment, which is merely the lid on his passion and rage. Critics have complained that there is nothing to prepare an audience for Leone's sudden and violent outburst against his wife's lover in the last act, but this criticism reveals a misunderstanding of the character and of the play. Since Leone's intellectual calm is the result of suppressing his passion, it implies throughout the possibility of an outbreak; and it is this contrast which makes the rôle a perfect acting part. The misunderstanding is a typical result of the over-intellectual approach to Pirandello—it comes from taking the intellectual surface of the play for the play itself.

Leone's detachment is the only form of peace he can find, and it is a state near to death. This is even more clear from *The Pleasure of Honesty*. Here the dupe who makes dupes of his dupers is Baldovino, a bankrupt with philosophical leanings and, in character, a more severe version of Leone. Like him, he has been forced by great suffering to a position of philosophical detachment from life. Agata, a society woman, is pregnant and her lover is a married man. These two employ Baldovino to mend appearances by becoming her husband, but Agata intends to discredit and divorce him once the baby has been legitimately born. However, Baldovino insists on playing his rôle with such uncompromising honesty that he has soon undercut the pretence and has turned appearances into reality. He becomes to all intents and purposes the real father of the child and even, when she falls in love with him, the real husband of Agata. At this point Baldovino suddenly wants to give up the game and leave, and this is where the Pirandellian position can be seen at its clearest. Baldovino knows that the genuine affection which he is beginning to feel for Agata will turn the game he is playing so perfectly into torture. For once, however, there is a happy ending. Agata comes away with him, leaving her old life behind her; and so Baldovino is brought back to life. He himself stresses the split between clear-seeing intellectual detachment from life and its opposite, a confusing involvement in life, in his remark:

When a man lives, he lives and does not see himself live.
I see because I came into this house not to live.[22]

The agony of passionate being and the death of intellectual
not-being—Pirandello found one extreme too painful and the
other too futile. But he did respect a middle way of compromise,
a sort of fantasy existence invented, like Professor Toti's
marriage, for charitable reasons. In *Cap and Bells* (1917) an employer is having an affair with his clerk's wife. His own wife
discovers this and lays a careful plot so that the clerk cannot
avoid finding the couple *in flagrante delicto*. The clerk is shattered
—not because he knew nothing of the affair, but precisely
because he did know about it and had intentionally kept his
knowledge secret. He loved his beautiful wife and thought
himself so ugly that he was content even to be her cuckold. But
now society expects histrionics from him: certainly his marriage
must break up. In his agony he thinks of a solution. He
persuades everyone that his employer's wife, who has
announced the scandalous news, is insane with unfounded
jealousy. She is taken off to a lunatic asylum and the tender and
valuable lie is preserved. The clerk has behaved with the same
wisdom beyond conventional morality as Professor Toti's. In
each case the lie was a charitable one and must be respected.

Pirandello had used a similar theme in *Right You Are, If You
Think So!* (1916), one of his two finest plays. A group of town
gossips is agog over the odd behaviour of three people, a
husband, his mother-in-law and his wife. Signor Ponza prevents
his mother-in-law, Signora Frola, from seeing her daughter and
yet spends much of his own time in his mother-in-law's house.
The explanations of this given by Signor Ponza and Signora
Frola are very strange and mutually contradictory. Each claims
that the other is mad, but that this madness must be respected.
Factually their stories clash over the identity of Signora Ponza,
the wife. The mother-in-law says this woman is his first wife and
her daughter; the husband claims that she is his second wife
and therefore not her daughter. Yet neither of them wants to
convince the other of his or her own version. As the gossips pry
deeper, the facts get no clearer but the suffering of the victims

becomes much more evident. They have found this way of living their lives together and it must be respected. In the final scenes Signora Ponza says:

> There is a misfortune here, as you see, which must stay hidden; otherwise the remedy which our compassion has found cannot avail.[23]

And Signor Ponza has already pleaded: 'For pity's sake, let them leave us in peace!' 'For pity's sake' is a phrase often repeated in Pirandello's plays. It is as central to the whole body of his work as 'the remedy which our compassion has found' is to this play.

Besides projecting the suffering of these central characters, the play satirizes the town gossips with their elaborate deductions from insufficient evidence. The audience, too, becomes subtly implicated in this satire (thus strengthening Pirandello's protest), because the play depends for its effect on our sharing the attitude of the gossips. We, like them, are fascinated to discover the 'real truth', but the final discovery gets us no further. Signora Ponza, the crucial character, appears for the first time at the end of the play, merely to announce that she is both Signor Ponza's second wife and Signora Frola's daughter —until now the only two certain opposites in the investigation. She adds that she is 'the one that people believe me to be'. This is what is important—her subjective relationship with other people, not the bare facts. The curtain comes down on the mocking laughter of Laudisi, the only cynical character. This 'twist' ending is typically Pirandellian, but it fails to twist quite far enough. The final impression is of the paradox that truth is illusory, whereas it should be that the truth is unimportant— especially when set against the compassionate lie. Pirandello, knowing how much his play depended for its effect on the intellectual paper-chase, called it *Right You Are, If You Think So!* In doing so he himself helped critics to lay too much stress on the play as a discussion of truth. The play might be better described by some such title as *The Remedy*.

But that again is too simple and inclines too much the other way. The power of Pirandello's theatre depends on the tug between these two elements—the intellectual comedy, and the passionate tragedy set in it like a burning scar. The intellectual comedy by itself would become tiresome, and in one or two plays, where it is predominant, does become so. The suffering by itself, concentrated on and wept over for its own sake, would become either pathos or melodrama; but, revealed bit by bit in its fierce struggle against intrusion or misinterpretation, it approaches tragedy. The struggle between these elements is Pirandello's theatre, and if the emphasis is tipped too far to one side by directors or critics, the essence of it is lost.

Six Characters in Search of an Author (1921) is Pirandello's most famous play and his best. It arises out of these earlier ones and adds another dimension to them. At the start a Producer and some Actors are on the stage rehearsing an earlier play of Pirandello's, *The Rules of the Game*. Six strange people suddenly arrive and tell the Producer that they are Characters created by an author, but then denied permanent life and form by him because he never completed their play. They now want the Producer to allow them to work out their story and present it in his theatre. Reluctant and bewildered, he agrees to let them try. From this point the central part of the action becomes the fight between the main Characters to impose on their story the interpretation and emphasis which suits each of them best. The facts turn out to be as follows:

> The Characters are the Father, the Mother, the Step-daughter, the Son, the Boy and the Little Girl. Many years ago the Father and the Mother were married and had one child, the Son. Later the Mother fell in love with the Father's secretary, and the Father sent her away to live with him. By him she had three children, the Stepdaughter, the Boy and the Little Girl. The Father, without being observed, tenderly watched these children growing up. He then lost track of them until, by a disastrous coincidence, he one day came face to face with the Stepdaughter, now aged seventeen. She was the girl given to him in a brothel, where she was working, without her mother's knowledge, to eke out the

family finances. The Father discovered her identity just in time. After that he took the family back to live in his own house, but events there led to the Little Girl's death by drowning in a fountain and to the Boy's suicide.

Pirandello describes *Six Characters* as 'A Play in the Making', and several different plays and interpretations, most of them very melodramatic, could be derived from these stark facts. The struggle between the Characters is to decide which the final version shall be. The Father, an intellectual, wants time to discuss and analyse his actions, hoping thereby partially to justify them. The Stepdaughter is determined to deny him this luxury; she feels that she has been degraded as far as is possible by the events and her one desire is to dwell on the sordid moments and so drag the Father down to her own level of nausea. Meanwhile the Mother, a passive sufferer, wants most of the story glossed over. In normal experience their interaction in front of the Producer would be nearest to that of a group of people who have been involved in a quarrel and who, in re-iterating it to an independent party, each try to bring him in on their side. Their dramatic narrative is constantly interrupted by the Actors who will eventually be playing their parts (which provides satirical comedy at the expense of the commercial theatre) and by the furious arguments between the Father and the Producer about the difference between human beings and fictional characters (comedy of ideas). However, they eventually complete their story and the play ends with a sudden and violent surprise. To the horror of the Actors, the Little Girl and the Boy are found to be really dead. This is not a cheap and sensational *coup de théâtre*, though it unfortunately may seem so to those members of the audience who, like the Actors on the stage, fail to see that it is the simple conclusion of the split between Character and Actor. At the end of his tragedy Hamlet the character is dead. It is the actor of Hamlet who rises, still covered in blood, to take his curtain call.

To the complexity of *Right You Are, If You Think So!*, *Six Characters* adds one extra dimension—that of art versus life—yet it is no less successful a whole than the earlier play. The two are surprisingly similar. *Six Characters* takes place, in a sense, one stage before *Right You Are*. Unlike the Ponzas and Signora Frola, the six Characters have not yet found their 'remedy', the final version of the facts by which they will live. The Ponzas had something to protect, and theirs became a drama of reticence. *Six Characters*, in which the leading Characters each want to have their own say, becomes the precise opposite, a drama of competitive revelatiᴄn. This in turn determines its strange and admirable dramatic form, with the characters 'demonstrating', in a very Brechtian manner, their experiences. One needs to see the play to realize the full dramatic effect of the Step-daughter's rushing through the scene in Madame Pace's brothel, skipping whole sections of it in her eagerness to reach the climax of degradation when she stands in the Father's arms.

At its simplest *Six Characters* is the drama of a play taking shape in a playwright's mind, 'a play in the making'. Pirandello has described in his Preface how these Characters, originally conceived for a novel and then discarded, kept returning to tempt and badger his mind (his rôle is, in this respect, taken in the play by the Producer) and the Stepdaughter also describes how she used to tempt the author in his study at night. So the play is, first of all, a dramatization of a direct experience, out of which the intellectual paradoxes arise—the precise opposite, once again, of drama as a vehicle for intellectual jugglery.

Pirandello wrote *Six Characters* in a burst of creative energy—it took him five days—and in the three preceding days he had written *Henry IV* (1921), which is often considered almost equally good. This judgement overrates it. The action takes place in a replica of Henry IV's court, and the hero's madness is that he believes himself to be Henry IV; but the drama comes from the fact that he became sane several years ago and could not then bring himself to take the painful step back into everyday life; so he continued, in self-protection, the pretence of madness. The play's main weakness is that the drama of its first act depends on our knowledge of what is not revealed till later—that he is sane. Without this knowledge the act seems a limp indulgence in pathos.

In his later plays Pirandello adopted a style nearer to Ibsen's, with less impressive results. *Naked* (1922) showed a girl being stripped of her protective lies, but the innumerable details of the plot tend to overwhelm the drama; and the girl's suffering, which in the earlier plays would have been touched on only at peak moments rising out of the comedy, is here given insistent and prolonged emphasis. The result is claustrophobic rather than dramatic. In *The Life I Gave You* (1924) and *Lazarus* (1929) Pirandello was trying to show fully rounded characters in detailed suffering. This, above all, is Ibsen's field and, though the plays are good, they fail to bring out the unique Pirandellian talent. He went to the opposite extreme in other plays, such as *Each in His Own Way* (1923), where the paradoxes are not grounded in any real human experience and so become facile and meaningless. In such a play as this, wilful intellectual contortions have carried Pirandello away. In it he comes nearest to what the world still thinks of as the real Pirandello. And it is a very bad play.

Pirandello once expressed well in an interview the real relationship between intellect and passion in his plays. He was talking about drama in general:

> The problems presented in a work of art are always problems of life . . . Take 'To be or not to be' out of the mouth of Hamlet, treat it as a philosophical problem, and you can solve it according to your own sweet fancy. But leave it there forever on Hamlet's lips, uttered out of his torment, and the question 'To be or not to be' will never be solved in all time. These life problems and emotions are imprisoned in a perfect form by a Shakespeare or a Dante, become fixed for eternity. Emotions embalmed alive.[24]

He could have been speaking of his own best plays. But critics, though they have refrained from taking 'To be or not to be' out of Hamlet's mouth, have treated Pirandello's dramatic arguments less respectfully. The Father in *Six Characters*, however much he may philosophize about the nature of reality, is finally brooding only on his own predicament, pleading his own case. The 'thoughts' are 'uttered out of his own torment', and that is their value. All Pirandello's good plays and all his successful characters can be summed up by the phrase 'emotions embalmed alive'—even if the emotion is almost invariably agony.

10

Eugene O'Neill 1888–1953

IF PIRANDELLO was the victim of being thought intellectual, O'Neill's troubles came from thinking himself so. His work suffered more than any other dramatist's from the general desire for 'significance'. His dramatic talent amounted to genius, but only within a very narrow framework—that of naturalistic drama; and only a fraction of O'Neill's output was naturalistic. The majority of his plays are top-heavy experiments, unable to support dramatically the load of meaning borrowed piecemeal from Nietzsche, Freud, Jung and Adler, and many of the books about his work appear to have been written by psychologists rather than literary critics. Fishing out O'Neill's sources and intentions makes a good academic parlour game, but critics sometimes forget how little their discoveries in this line have to do with dramatic merit. An extreme example of this is Oscar Cargill's pronouncement in *Intellectual America* that *Lazarus Laughed* is 'the supreme piece of drama of modern times', mainly on the grounds that it uses so fully the ideas which Jung set out in his *Psychological Types*. Cargill is undaunted by the fact that the play has had only one production in the thirty–odd years since its publication; 'we cannot believe that it exhausted the possibilities of the play', he comments. One would hope not, yet the lack of any other productions is understandable. The hero spends a large proportion of the play just laughing—sometimes alone, sometimes in harmony with a chorus of over a hundred people. Criticism can drift too far from the considerations of the theatre.

As a young man, in the years before he took up play-writing, O'Neill went through a period when his experience of the world must have been peculiarly intense. It was to provide him with material for most of his best work, the best of all, *Long Day's Journey into Night*, being written some thirty years after the events. His parents were devout Catholics, and his father, James O'Neill, was a touring actor-manager. The family travelled round the country with James O'Neill, but their home was unsettled in more ways than this. None of them were in good health, the father drank heavily and the mother took drugs. O'Neill himself was suspended from Princeton during his first year, and then spent a hectic five years doing a variety of jobs which included gold-mining in Honduras and travelling all over the world as a merchant-seaman. He was married, had a son, Eugene Jr., and was divorced. He spent several months as a bum around the docks of Buenos Aires, and several more on the waterfront in New York. During this time he lived and drank in a bar called Jimmy the Priest's, which was to be the model for Harry Hope's in *The Iceman Cometh*. This lacks only tuberculosis to be the traditional writer's apprenticeship, and O'Neill did, in 1912, contract the disease.

It was during his months of convalescence that he wrote his first short plays, and eleven of these were published together under the title *The Moon of the Caribbees* (1918). Most of them are mere sketches, catching at the authentic flavour of life at sea and in ports, but their merit is in the dialogue and characterization of the nine or ten sailors, of several different nationalities, who crop up throughout the series. These portraits of O'Neill's own shipmates are naturalism at its simplest and purest—they are the proper roots of O'Neill's talent.

But this was the age of experiment, and O'Neill found experiment irresistible. Nearly all his more famous works of the twenties are plays stretched on the rack of an idea. The few naturalistic scenes which they contain are invariably the best scenes. *The Emperor Jones* (1920) shows the downfall of a flamboyant negro criminal who has set himself up as the Emperor of a Caribbean island. In the first scene Smithers, a Cockney trader, gloatingly warns Jones that there is at last a rebellion against him in the hills, where the natives are already working themselves into a frenzy with their tom-toms. The remaining scenes follow Jones through the jungle, as he tries to make his escape. To the constant accompaniment of the tom-tom beat—it starts at the rate of a heart-beat and then grows steadily faster—the man stumbles on, haunted by apparitions. The first of these are 'black, shapeless' objects, called by O'Neill the Little Formless Fears. We are firmly in the realm of expressionism. The apparitions turn into the victims of his own past crimes and then, with no abrupt change, they plunge further back into the past of the negro race: Jones sees a slave-auction, and then a witch-doctor. O'Neill has switched from an expressionistic presentation of a guilty conscience to a 'clever' use of Jung's theory of the collective unconscious. In the theatre these scenes may be effective, though chiefly because of the tom-tom, which is little more than a gimmick, and not even a new gimmick—Austin Strong had used it several years before. But they compare very badly with the naturalistic first scene, in which the dialogue tight-ropes between possible explosions of rage. Smithers despises Jones for the colour of his skin but is genuinely afraid of him: he therefore likes to taunt him, but will cringe and wheedle when he has gone too far. Jones despises Smithers as a man but is vain enough to want to conceal from him how afraid he is. With this balance of power the dialogue can twist and turn between opposite extremes, and the relationship between the characters can remain fluid and dramatic. It is a form of writing which was O'Neill's particular strength. Patches of it enliven his unsuccessful plays and it is what makes *Long Day's Journey into Night* so outstanding.

The Hairy Ape (1922) takes a further step into expressionism, both in technique and in its disgust at modern humanity. The lower classes in it are hairy apes, the upper classes mere marionettes. Like Toller and Kaiser, O'Neill finds no glory in industrial labour but, unlike them, he cannot see a way back to nature. Yank, the hero, is a stoker who does not feel that he 'belongs' anywhere in modern society. He ends by envying the gorilla in the zoo, who is unable to think and is content with what he is. He opens the door of the cage and is hugged to death by the animal, which then (only an O'Neill ape could act with such proper symbolism) throws his body into the cage, closes the door and shuffles off. 'And, perhaps, the Hairy Ape at last belongs' is O'Neill's final comment.

It is hard to believe that even in his bleakest moments

O'Neill meant the full implications of this story. It gives, instead, the impression that his symbolism has run away with him. Early in the play Yank's fury and self-doubt are first aroused when a beautiful, rich woman describes him as a 'hairy ape', and the end is merely this idea carried to its logical conclusion, regardless of any sort of reality. There is evidence of similar empty intellectualism throughout the play. Yank, for instance, is frequently discovered in the position of Rodin's *The Thinker*. This is an example of the type of theatrical short-hand which O'Neill was later to use extensively in the form of psychological catchphrases; but at least it has, to begin with, a clear and ironical meaning, since Yank's troubles started when he tried to think about himself. But then, to one's amazement, one discovers the gorilla in the zoo in the same position, whereas the whole symbolic point about this creature is that he does not think (Yank says this), but merely belongs. The meaning of the Rodin theme tumbles to the ground.

The original set of O'Neill's next play, *All God's Chillun Got Wings* (1923), accurately reflected the weakness of his work at this time. The play is about the way the racial problem oppresses a mixed couple, the wife white and the husband black, until she is driven insane and drags him back to a state resembling childhood—the only level on which they had ever been able properly to meet. Some of the scenes take place on the corner between a white street and a negro street. The New York set had on one side houses drawn with thin black lines on a pure white background, and on the opposite side houses drawn with thin white lines on a black background. In the photograph this looks both magnificent and significant, but the actors are hardly distinguishable in front of it. The people have been lost in the idea.

With *Desire under the Elms* (1924) (I have already described its plot in detail on page 92) O'Neill made a sudden but, unfortunately, temporary break with his intellectual and stylistic experiments. Using a simple naturalistic form he achieved in this play the highest imaginative peak of his career. His other plays of a comparable stature were all direct and painful distillations of his own experience, and they are at their best when they come nearest in every detail to that experience. *Desire under the Elms* is pure imaginative creation, no nearer to the everyday realities of O'Neill's life than *Phèdre* was to Racine's, yet also no less real than *Phèdre*. The psychological patterns are present in this play for critics to dig out, but they are deep down, an integral part of the dramatic situation, as in *Hamlet* or *Oedipus Rex*. A spectator who fails to notice them will not notice his failure. They are the hidden and mysterious depths of a human action, instead of a series of rocks marked out on a sea chart.

Unfortunately, O'Neill's charting period had not even reached its prime. His next three plays are all frameworks forged to contain ideas, and are more blatantly patterned than anything he had yet written. *The Great God Brown* (1926) is an allegory of the battle between the ascetic and the dionysiac, and between the artist (in whom both these elements are warring) and the materialism of society. O'Neill has attempted to express the various contrasts by the use of masks, which his characters take on and off as the situation requires. On a simple level this trick makes sense. A character can validly take off his mask when he is alone and then put it on again when he has to face the world. The masks could even be used very sparingly for a more complicated purpose—such as one character finding another with his mask off when he first becomes aware of the other's more secret personality—*but only if* the discovery has also been made on the level of realism, by a remark perhaps, or by an action. Without this anchor in reality the use of masks becomes a mere substitute for the drama—an echo without a shout, a code-number for an unwritten story. O'Neill uses his masks without any anchor, and to such excess that his trick topples into pure nonsense. At one point a character steals another's mask from him after his death and so takes his place at his wife's side without her noticing. From that point on much of the dramatic interest centres on his attempts to avoid being found in the wrong place with the wrong mask on. When he is caught with his mask down he has to hurry out of the room to put it on before re-entering as, ostensibly, another person. We are in a world of farce, except that there the masks would be trousers. Reality is quite forgotten. The allegory itself is watertight and can therefore be interpreted satisfactorily on a general level—i.e. by deducing from it the abstract generalities about personality from which O'Neill so carefully constructed it. Thus the dead man and the spoiler of his corpse are, of course, two halves of the same person. But this is an *Alice in Wonderland* occupation—it has nothing to do with drama. Try to take the step back from watertight logic to human reality, and, like Alice, you flounder. This play is what Pirandello would be like if his critics were right about him. It is the extreme example of O'Neill's particular failings and, even apart from the masks, reveals constantly his intellectual pretentiousness. The warm prostitute, for example, in whose mothering lap Dion Anthony (libertine Dionysus, ascetic St Anthony) lays his head, is called Cybel—because she represents Cybele, the Earth Mother. In her parlour the pianola grinds out 'mammy' tunes; and it has 'cheap wall-paper of a dull yellow-brown, resembling a blurred impression of a fallow field in early spring'.

Lazarus Laughed and *Marco Millions* (both 1928) are less abstruse than *The Great God Brown*, though still purely intellectual in concept. *Lazarus Laughed* requires more than two hundred and fifty different masks, and almost every scene follows an identical pattern—that of Lazarus disarming his powerful opponents by his laughter. If *The Emperor Jones* had the excitement of a chase, and *The Great God Brown* the complications of a farce, Lazarus' unfailing escapes from disaster have the quality of Superman in a comic: however startling O'Neill's ideas, his dramatizations of them follow old-enough patterns. *Marco Millions* is a better play than either of the others, because it is simpler and contains some good satirical touches at the expense of mammon, but there is still the rigid patterning. One lavish scene is repeated three times, with only the slightest differences, in order to show the changes in Marco Polo as he grows older.

After *Lazarus Laughed* and *Marco Millions*, both of which demand extravagant productions, O'Neill's thoughts turned to a different type of grandeur. *Strange Interlude* (1928) is three times the length of a normal play, chiefly because the characters speak their thoughts as well as their words. O'Neill sometimes achieves good effects by this method—as when a character in his thoughts misinterprets another's remark, with the result that we, who know the right interpretation, are made to see the reason for the mistake—but in general it is ponderous. His next attempt aims even higher—at being a modern tragedy to rival the Greek masterpieces, no less.

This was the trilogy, *Mourning becomes Electra* (1931), in which O'Neill tried to write a version of the Orestes story which would be as relevant to the twentieth century as Aeschylus's *Oresteia* was to Athens. His method was to transplant the story to New England at the time of the Civil War, and to give sexual motivation to every twist of the plot. His result was merely to belittle his archetypes. Where Clytaemnestra had exulted with a fierce magnificence in her murder of Agamemnon, Christine Mannon's murder of Ezra is a sordid boudoir affair which is brought to light only when Lavinia (the Electra of the story) accidentally finds a box of poisonous pills. Orin Mannon (Orestes) takes time, after murdering Brant (Aegisthus), to fabricate evidence which makes the deed look like the work of thieves. O'Neill has taken out the Furies and brought in the police.

The sexual motivations might possibly succeed if O'Neill used them less openly or carried them less far. As with his other ideas, from the hairy ape to the masks of *The Great God Brown*, he goes to extremes. The Mannon troubles revolve round three incestuous attractions inside the family; father-daughter, mother-son, brother-sister. Leaving aside homosexuality, the canon is complete. Lavinia's emotional involvements, if one separates them from the mesh of the play, turn out to be as follows: she hates her mother, loves her father, loves her brother, loves Brant, her mother's lover, and in moments of confusion sees her brother as Brant and herself as her mother and therefore hates her father and desires his death, as her mother did. Even so, all this might be tolerable if O'Neill had merely left it implicit. Instead he makes the characters themselves express it. So Christine says to her daughter:

You've tried to become the wife of your father and the mother of Orin! You've always schemed to steal my place.

Christine admits that she fell in love with Brant only because he reminded her of her son, and Orin admits that he flirted with a girl only so as to make his mother jealous. It is this pat admission of their Freudian impulses which makes these characters ludicrous. Once again O'Neill is signposting, using a modern shorthand, writing from outside. In several scenes the authentic O'Neill style, the dramatic muscularity of the first scene of *The Emperor Jones*, begins to reappear; but it is soon swamped again by the ideas. A character in *Strange Interlude* said that 'Herr Freud' had 'a lot to account for'—not the least of which is this period of Eugene O'Neill's work. Looking back over the plays, with all the men putting their heads in their mistresses' laps and calling them mother, one can validly wish that the characters would stop behaving, within their given framework, with such predictable conventionality.

Mourning becomes Electra failed to be a monument, but it did in a sense become a tomb for the O'Neill of this period. After it he wrote one Christian play, *Days without End*, and one period comedy, *Ah, Wilderness!* (both 1934) neither of them particularly interesting. For the next twelve years no new O'Neill play appeared. The playwright who then emerged was a much more impressive figure. He had gone back to the methods and material of his earliest plays.

The Iceman Cometh (1946) takes place in a bums' bar. The alcoholics who drink there all have 'pipe-dreams' of returning to the busy and responsible world outside, and the play concerns their attempt, and failure, to do so. Its value lies in the very varied characters of these down-and-outs, in their attitudes to one another and to the outside world, in their quarrels, their interdependence, their pretences, their kindness, their hopes and their fears. All these combine to produce an almost poetic evocation, even though the play is naturalistic, of futility and of the comfort of having other people to be futile with. But the play has its faults. Traces of O'Neill's intellectualism remain, in the patterning of certain scenes and in some disastrously counterpointed speeches; and there is an unresolved confusion in the rôle and character of Hickey. He is the travelling salesman who makes the bums take the step into the outside world. He has, he says, done the equivalent in his own life, and they, like him, will experience a great sense of freedom once they have tried and failed (he knows that they will fail, though he does not tell them this) to put their pipe-dreams into effect. However, instead of feeling free, they merely become depressed. Nothing can revive them, not even liquor, until they discover that Hickey is mad and can therefore be disregarded. His liberating action, it turns out, was the murder of his wife.

Throughout the play the audience has been taking Hickey at his face value. He seems simply the prime mover of the plot, which is all that he needs to be since all the emphasis is on the bums. Now the audience suddenly needs to reconsider him and, in retrospect, the whole of the play. To do so is fairly difficult, particularly in the theatre, and O'Neill complicates matters by failing to stress why Hickey's experience is essentially irrelevant to the bums. He killed his wife because he could not bear the guilt of deceiving her and the indignity of being forgiven by her. He has always claimed to be a cynic, whom nothing could touch, even joking that his wife was sleeping with the iceman, but this was a pretence. In this he is like the only bum whom he changes, his one 'convert to death', Larry Slade. Slade is an ex-revolutionary, who claims to care about nothing any more but who really drinks to drown his disgust with himself. His illusion, like Hickey's, was that he felt no guilt, whereas the illusion of the others is that they do feel guilt: they are in reality content with their existence and pretend that it is temporary only so as to let it become permanent. No wonder, then, that Hickey's experience is irrelevant to the others. *The Iceman Cometh* would be a better play if this violent contrast between him and the rest were either omitted or else properly dealt with. As it is, it tends to obscure the play's real and excellent centre—the drifting drama of the bums.

In O'Neill's remaining plays the patterning and intellectualism is quite done away with. *Moon for the Misbegotten* (written 1943, produced 1957) and *A Touch of the Poet* (written 1943, produced 1958) both contain good scenes, though neither is fully successful. *Moon for the Misbegotten* has too much of the routine *comédie d'intrigue* about it, and *A Touch of the Poet* sprawls. It does, though, have something of the ambivalence of character which had reached its peak in *Long Day's Journey into Night* (written 1940–1, produced 1956).

Very little happens in *Long Day's Journey into Night*. It concerns the attempts of O'Neill's own family, here called the Tyrones, to live together. The immediate problem is that the mother, a temporarily cured drug-addict, may revert because her younger son, Edmund, may have T.B. It is therefore vital that she should be protected, and so the recriminations which are constantly welling up are fought down by the family's need to care for her. Scene by scene, even moment by moment, the drama veers between love and hate, between fury and precarious calm.

In this play O'Neill achieved all that he had been moving towards in his others. The constant see-sawing of the relationship between characters dates from as far back as the first scene of *The Emperor Jones*. The multiple aspects of personality, which in the masks of *The Great God Brown* had been mere idea-mongering, are here presented naturalistically and movingly. So the mother, left alone on the stage by her family, says to herself:

> It's so lonely here. (*Then her face hardens into self-contempt.*) You're lying to yourself again. You wanted to get rid of them. Their contempt and disgust aren't pleasant company. You're glad they're gone. (*She gives a little despairing laugh.*) Then Mother of God, why do I feel so lonely?

The changes of mask are properly buried here in the language. And the unbreakable entanglement of these characters with one another, which in *Mourning becomes Electra* O'Neill had tried to forge artificially by means of Freud, is now achieved quite simply by a network of recriminations. They all hate the mother for her weakness; she hates her husband for never having given her a fixed home and she hates her elder son because she blames him for the death of her youngest child; the sons hate the miserly father for having employed a cheap doctor whose irresponsible use of drugs on their mother started her addiction

—and so on. And yet they all love one another. Even the drinking and the illusion-guarding of *The Iceman Cometh* achieve a more coherent expression here. The family cling to their illusions— the mother does not want anyone to fetch the result of Edmund's T.B. test, because she refuses to face the possible truth, and they all avoid noticing that she is slipping back to her drugs. Gradually they fall back on drink as a refuge.

Their intoxication, paradoxically, raises the level of the play and the last scene is the peak of O'Neill's art. The grandeur, which he had sought throughout his plays, he now found in the drama of his own home; partly because the depth of his family's suffering creates its own grandeur, and partly through a trick which rises naturalistically out of the situation and which therefore seems no trick. In their cups these naturalistic characters can justifiably expand, philosophize, dramatize. As he grows more drunk, Edmund, who 'has the makings of a poet', pronounces on all that he loves and loathes in life. Soon he and his brother are quoting their favourite poetry, first Baudelaire and then the fashionable poets of romantic despair, Wilde, Symons, Dowson. The play steadily rises above its original level of naturalism, without ever breaking that convention. It adopts grandeur from the borrowed lines and then tinges it with the irony of its own sordid context. Finally the mother drifts in, dragging her wedding-dress, which she has just dug out of her trunk. She is in a drugged daze of memories. Her last line contains the whole irony and pity of it all. She is rummaging confusedly through memories of her young life in a convent, and of the Mother Superior who had advised her to go out into the world and enjoy parties and dances before becoming a nun. She says:

> I never dreamed Holy Mother would give me such advice! . . . That was in the winter of senior year. Then in the spring something happened to me. Yes, I remember. I fell in love with James Tyrone and was so happy for a time.

(curtain)

The general attitude to O'Neill is strangely ambivalent—he is approached with a peculiar mixture of veneration and distaste. Allardyce Nicoll in *World Drama* accords him greatness and then finds reasons for dismissing almost all his plays, and a chapter heading in Bentley's *In Search of Theatre* effectively sums up the dichotomy—'Trying to like O'Neill'. The reason is that O'Neill always demanded serious attention because he so constantly threatened the stage with high astounding terms—which then often turned out to be mere bombast. With such extremes of quality in his work it is essential to separate ruthlessly the successful from the merely ambitious. For O'Neill was like the proverbial child—when he was good, he was very very good.

II

Bertolt Brecht 1898–1956

MORAL paradox is at the root of Brecht's theatre. It arises throughout his plays from the clash between ends and means, between the intention and the effect, between the individual and the world. The Communist agent who has to be cruel to be kind; Mother Courage, who has to deny one child to save another; Azdak, who is so corrupt that he is incorruptible; Puntila, who is tolerable only when he is drunk; Galileo, whose unscrupulous dishonesty makes his research possible and whose betrayal of the truth then makes it useless—these are the typical Brechtian characters.

His plays fall into three clear chronological groups. There are the earliest, written in the wild and whirling spirit of the twenties, full of excitement but lacking control, mixing satire and indulgence almost inextricably. The most famous of these is *The Threepenny Opera*. Then there are, in violent contrast, the 'didactic' plays of the early thirties—cool, stark and precise. And, finally, the major plays, which combine the best of the two earlier styles and which were all written in a burst of creative energy before and during the Second World War.

Brecht's first play, *Baal* (1918), takes a romantic plunge into anarchy. Its images are as wildly exuberant as its characters; there are swirling rivers, clouds scudding across open skies, winds tearing at the trees, while the energetic wenching of the two heroes does nothing to lessen their homosexual love for each other. If *Baal* rejected romanticism by debasing it, *Drums in the Night* (1922), Brecht's first performed play, did the same by treating normally romantic subjects—a soldier's homecoming, marriage, revolution—with total cynicism. The soldier returns to find his fiancée pregnant, leaves her in disgust to fight in the Communist uprising in Munich, becomes even more disillusioned there and so comes back to marry her. There were

placards in the auditorium saying: 'Don't stare so roman-
tically.' Like Toller, Brecht was involved in the Munich uprising
but he did not, during the twenties, share Toller's faith in the
party.

Drums in the Night won Brecht the Kleist Prize, but it was *The
Threepenny Opera* (1928), very loosely based on Gay's *The Beggar's
Opera*, which made him famous. It is not quite the pungent
masterpiece which it is sometimes claimed to be, and its satire
scores far less accurately than Gay's. Gay parodied the immoral
ruling class of his time in the figures of Macheath, Peachum and
Lockit, the aristocracy of the criminal classes. Brecht, far less
aptly, was intending similar criminals to stand for the capitalist
bourgeoisie—whose vices are, in sober fact, less flamboyant.
The Threepenny Opera's great and lasting success is due to Brecht's
caustic lyrics, to the superb irony of various individual (and
therefore quotable) lines, and to the jangling charm of Kurt
Weill's music. *The Rise and Fall of Mahagonny City* (1929), an opera by
the same team, directed its satire more carefully but lacked some
of the vitality of *The Threepenny Opera*.

Up till 1929 Brecht's plays had shown almost as little direction
as the society which he was satirizing, but the rising threat of
Nazism now swung him to the other extreme—to a fanatical
embracing of the certainties of Communism. He began his
series of 'didactic' plays (*Lehrstücke*), designed for performance in
schools. Each of these sets out to clarify some aspect of life or
Communism, but almost invariably it is moral paradox which
they reveal. So *The Horatii and the Curatii* (1934) proves that the
soldier who wins is the one who breaks the code of honour and
runs away at the strategic moment. In *The Exception and the Rule*
(1930) the Merchant shoots the Coolie who is offering him a
drink in the desert—he mistook the water-bottle for a stone and
the offer for an attack. So the Merchant, to prove his plea of
self-defence, finds himself in the very paradoxical position of
having to prove to the judge that the Coolie had every reason to
hate him. In *The Measures Taken* (1930) a young Communist is
killed by his comrades: his vice was his practising of the normal
virtues, such as sympathy and honesty, because his sympathy
for individual sufferers and his protests against isolated cases of

injustice were endangering the wider Communist cause. The opposite paradox is the central idea of *The Seven Deadly Sins* (1933) (not a didactic play, but a ballet with songs written during this period), in which a young girl's apparent avoidance of vice is, on closer inspection, a careful avoidance of virtue. Eschewing the seven deadly sins turns out greatly to help young Anna to earn the money which her Puritan and bourgeois relations need to build their little house—she gives up the Pride which had prevented her from stripping in a night-club, fights down the Anger which she feels at the sight of injustice, and so on through all the seven sins.

These didactic plays are chiefly interesting because it was in them that Brecht fully discovered his own style of theatre, the style on which he was to base his major plays. Their starkness and simplicity make them the clearest exemplars of this style. At the end of *The Exception and the Rule* the players comment:

> We beseech you then:
> Whatever is not strange, find that the strangest,
> Whatever is usual, find inexplicable.

The German for 'strange' is '*fremd*', and these lines express the intention of Brecht's famous *Verfremdungseffekt*—usually referred to in English as the 'Alienation Effect'.

The intention of this 'making strange' was to force the audience to respond intellectually to the action of the play and to question it, instead of responding emotionally and accepting it. To achieve this end Brecht thought it would be sufficient to break the 'illusion' of the theatre, by which the spectators can become so engrossed in a play that they temporarily forget where they are, and the most obvious techniques of the Alienation Effect were all devised to remind the audience that it is sitting in a theatre. So Brecht left the stage apparatus visible, presented a synopsis of each scene on a placard, or had narrators talking directly to the audience. It is by now a commonplace that his techniques failed, fortunately, to eliminate the audience's emotional involvement with the characters; and it

is one of the major paradoxes about Brecht that instead of
inspiring, as he intended, a simple working-class audience to
dispassionate thought, he moved and excited an international
audience of intellectuals. This 'failure' was the result of a
misjudgement in Brecht's theory. He was wrong to equate
empathy, one of the oldest elements of theatre and almost
certainly inseparable from it, with illusion—which is a relative
upstart, being the peculiar property of Naturalism. It was
in fact Naturalism against which all Brecht's technique was
directed, and his theatre therefore has stylistic similarities with
much of pre-naturalistic drama. There is 'alienation' in Greek
Tragedy, in medieval Mystery plays, in the Nō plays, in
Jacobean drama. Even etchings of Molière's own company
in performance look strangely similar. to Brecht's Berliner
Ensemble. None of these earlier theatres relied on illusion, yet
they all caused emotional involvement. One should add, in
fairness, that Brecht's theorizing was often inconsistent and that
he has been frequently represented by his most extreme statements, whereas once, for example, when describing *The Mother*,
which conforms more nearly to his theories than most of his
plays, he admitted that it merely used the emotional involvement of the spectator 'less unhesitatingly' than the work of
other playwrights. And late in his life, confronted with his
inconsistencies, he wearily made the very sympathetic protest:
'I cannot rewrite all the notes to my plays.'[25]

More interesting than the technical aspects of the Alienation
Effect, such as leaving the stage machinery visible, is its effect
on Brecht's dialogue; and, through the dialogue, on the style
of acting of his company. A naturalistic scene achieves its
purposes obliquely—an essential piece of exposition, for
example, will be introduced so subtly and naturally that the
audience is unaware that it is being 'told' anything. Brecht,
desiring clarity and distrusting the oblique approach, starts in
directly with the essence of his scene. His characters state
immediately, and baldly, whatever is necessary. In *The Mother*
(1932), his adaptation of Gorki's novel, four comrades come
to Pawel's house to print pamphlets. Pawel lives with his
mother, who has urged him not to take part in these

dangerous revolutionary activities. The scene opens as follows:

> *Four young workers, one of them a woman, come early in the morning*
> *with a mimeograph machine.*
>
> Anton Rybin: When you joined our movement a few weeks
> ago, Pawel, you said that we could come here if there was
> any special job to be done. Your house is the safest place,
> since we have never worked here.
>
> Pawel Wlassow: What do you want to do?
>
> Andrej Nachodka: We must get leaflets printed today. The
> recent wage-cuts have violently stirred up the workers.
> For three days we have been distributing leaflets in the
> factory. Today is the vital day. This evening at the general
> meeting it will be decided whether we accept the cut of
> one kopek or whether we strike.
>
> Iwan Wassowtschikow: We have brought the mimeograph
> machine and the paper.
>
> Pawel: Sit down. My mother will make us tea.

A revealing contrast to this stark functionalism is the version of
the play made for a New York production by Paul Peters, who
had written with George Sklar the successful *Stevedore*. Brecht
objected violently, and understandably, to this New York
version. The printing scene in it begins:

> *There is a knock on the door. Pawel gets up quickly. The mother*
> *surprised, turns and watches him. A small group of revolutionary workers,*
> *enters. Several of them have bulges under their coats.*
>
> Anton Rybin: Well, here we are.
>
> Pawel: Hello, Anton! Andrei!
>
> Masha (*looking round*): Yes, it looks safe here. They'll never
> find us here.
>
> Andrei: This is Masha Chalatova, Pawel. (*They shake hands.*)
> Pawel just joined us last week. And this is Ivan, Ivan
> Vessovchikov. Pawel offered us his home, when there was
> special work to do.
>
> (*more handshaking*)
>
> Ivan: There's plenty of that, all right.

Andrei: We've got to print leaflets today, Pawel. That wage-cut has set the whole plant on its ear. We've been passing leaflets out the last three days.

Masha: But today's the day that counts.

Andrei: There's going to be a shop-meeting tonight to decide whether we let them get away with it—or strike!

Anton: So—(*he pulls out a mimeograph machine from under his coat and holds it up*)—we brought our little printing plant along.

(*Masha pulls out several reams of paper from under her coat. They all laugh.*)

Pawel (*laughing with them*): Sit down. Sit down. Mother will make some tea for you.

To make the scene more 'real', Peters has draped it in a thin cloak of naturalism—the slang phrases, the greetings, the handshakes with the necessary gobbets of exposition concealed neatly between them, and even the small life-like touches in the stage-directions. To make it more sympathetic he has introduced the friendly little jokes, such as 'there's plenty of that, all right', or 'our little printing plant'. And to make it more dramatic he has resorted to melodrama, with the bulges under the coats and such phrases as 'whether we let them get away with it—or strike!' Some of the ill-effects of this are immediately obvious. He has almost doubled the length of the scene. He has made particular what in Brecht was general, and has replaced Brecht's clear formality with a nauseating and sentimental air of camaraderie. (Ionesco has dismissed Brecht's plays as being 'Boy Scout', but there can be no doubt which of these two extracts is nearer to the true Baden Powell spirit.) Also he has made aspects of the scene totally false. For example, one of the new arrivals tells another (for the benefit of the audience) that Pawel has offered them his home to work in—a fact which the man could hardly have helped picking up on his way here. And what conspirators walk around with bulges under their coats rather than a suitcase?

But there remains one flaw in Peters' version much deeper than these. He has totally obscured the real dramatic content of Brecht's scene. Even in reading the Brecht lines, and much more so in seeing them, it is clear that the central drama of the scene is Pawel's decision. Will he let them use his house or not? The others state the facts to him, while he merely stands there and asks the relevant question: 'What do you want to do?' His subsequent: 'Sit down. My mother will make us tea' is unmistakably his decision, his acceptance of involvement. Brecht's scene, with the whole group focussed on Pawel, requires no movement on the stage: Peters' implies a constant bustle, in which Pawel will be quite lost. So, by putting all the emphasis on the surface reality, on characterization and on titillating the audience's interest, Peters has ruined the scene. Brecht's original is more economical, more clear, more dramatic and, the final paradox, more moving. This paradox was one particularly useful by-product of the Alienation Effect. Designed to withdraw spectators far enough away from a commonplace moral situation so that they could view it in a fresh light, it had the effect of withdrawing them far enough to respond freshly to commonplace emotional situations, which would be real enough to them in life but which in art they would, from over-familiarity, reject as 'corny'. An analogy is the beautiful sunset which becomes nauseating when reproduced by a naturalistic painter. With the formality derived from his Alienation Effect Brecht was able to return to the most basic emotional situations. *The Caucasian Chalk Circle* would be intolerably sentimental if adapted by Peters.

In a sense, of course, Peters' version of the scene from *The Mother* is the more life-like. Conspirators would greet each other. Brecht, interested only in the inner realism of the scene, has written totally non-naturalistic dialogue. It would be almost impossible for actors to perform it naturalistically—the script itself demands the style of acting which Brecht wanted. His descriptions of this style are well known. He said that an actor must 'demonstrate' his part. He must remain outside the character, criticizing him and always emphasizing that he could be taking the opposite decision—as Pawel could. Such acting is similar to a person in real life describing, and enacting, a quarrel which he has witnessed. To help his actors, Brecht made them use the narrative third-person during rehearsals.

So the actor playing Pawel would say: 'Then Pawel asked, What do you want to do?' and this description by an actor of his rôle often remains, in various forms, in the text of Brecht's plays. The wealthy chemist in *The Good Woman of Setzuan*, after making his sordid proposal to Shen Te, goes out saying:

> And now I go, quietly and modestly, making no claims, on tiptoe, full of veneration, selflessly.[26]

Even reading this line one can vizualize precisely the Brechtian style of acting which it demands, though once again the clearest example of all comes from one of the didactic plays. In *The Measures Taken* the four agitators enact before the court the series of actions by their comrade which led up to their decision to kill him. In each successive scene a different one of the four plays the comrade's rôle. All four understood his actions, and yet disapproved of them; therefore, if even the most determined naturalistic actor were playing one of the agitators, he would inevitably find himself performing in a Brechtian style when it became his turn to represent the comrade—for he would have to retain the independent personality and critical attitude of the agitator, just as the actor of any other Brechtian rôle has to retain his own personality and attitude

The dramatic style developed in the didactic plays was to be the basis, once he had broadened his terms of reference and added flesh to his characters, of Brecht's four major plays. The characters in *He Who Said Yes* (1930) lamented 'the sorrowful ways of the world', though their play, like the other didactic plays, deals with only one very specific instance of these ways. The sorrowful ways of the world still dominate the major plays; but now the central characters suffer them in a much broader and more general context.

'Whatever there is shall go to those who are good for it.' This is the theme of *The Caucasian Chalk Circle* (1948). An Empress deserts her baby son during a revolution, and a young kitchen-maid, Grusha, reluctantly rescues the child. She knows the risk she takes in protecting a prince, but 'terrible is the temptation of goodness' comments the story-teller. The first half of the play shows her difficulties as she trudges through the countryside, trying to escape from the Ironshirts. Her greatest dilemma and misery comes in the last scene. She is washing clothes in a stream when her soldier fiancé returns from the wars. He is on the other side of the stream (two rows of reeds down the centre of the stage), and in their embarrassment they greet each other across it with true Brechtian reserve—speaking, in fact, mainly in proverbs. Then he sees the child's cap in the grass. She is just explaining that the little boy is not hers, when two Ironshirts arrive with him. 'Is this your child?' they ask. 'Yes,' she replies, and then immediately shouts out 'Simon!' to her fiancé as he turns to stride away. In the event she loses both of them, because the Ironshirts arrest the boy on suspicion. She is left shambling after them and crying: 'He is mine. He is mine.'

In the second half of the play we meet Azdak, a magnificently roguish fellow who has accidentally become a judge during the revolution. He is so corrupt that he will even take bribes from a plaintiff and then pronounce the verdict against him, but his judgements have a Robin Hood type of justice which delves below the letter of the law. In the case between the Empress and Grusha, at the end of the play, he awards the child to Grusha, the mother who is good for it. By implication Azdak's scenes are an attack on conventional law, since no other judge would have pronounced in favour of Grusha, but Brecht does not stress this. He allows the scenes to be as simply and hugely enjoyable as the Rabelaisian character of Azdak makes them, just as Grusha's scenes had been moving in the obstinate simplicity of her struggles to protect the child.

Shen Te, the heroine of *The Good Woman of Setzuan* (1943), suffers, like Grusha, for her goodness. The gods give her a reward of a thousand dollars for it, but this only complicates her life. She is soon almost ruined by the crowds of people who begin to depend on her. To protect herself she dresses up as the fierce Shui Ta, supposedly her male cousin, and in this disguise quickly tidies up her affairs. She starts a factory in which the most unpleasant characters rise to positions of power and cause great misery. So tough Shui Ta is soon hated while generous Shen Te finds life impossible. The gods, with a smile of goodwill,

E

leave her to solve her dilemma. Brecht does the same, but
with a question mark.

Grusha and Shen Te are passive sufferers, pure victims of
'the sorrowful ways of the world'. Mother Courage and Galileo
also suffer, but they are both partly responsible for the state of
the world and for their own suffering. Mother Courage (*Mother
Courage*, 1941) is a *vivandière* in the Thirty Years' War. She deeply
loves her children and yet she profiteers from the war which
kills all three of them. The tragic irony which results from this
dichotomy in her life becomes complete in the last scene of the
play. The wagon, which at the start was swarming with activity
—two sons pulling it, herself and her daughter on the box—is
now bleak and empty. But it is all that she has left. As the
curtain falls, a column of troops passes by. Laboriously she heaves
it off to join them—back to the way of life which has ruined her,
but the only one she knows.

Her story contains moments of agonizing dilemma, similar
to Grusha's by the stream. At one point the enemy soldiers who
have just killed her son bring his corpse to her. If she acknow-
ledges him, her life and her daughter's may be in danger;
certainly she will no longer be able to do business with this
new conquering army. She stands completely still while they
uncover the body and merely shakes her head to their questions.
Finally the sergeant-major orders the soldiers: 'Dump him in
the knacker's pit. He has no one who knows him.' This short
scene contains the essence of the play; it is precise and moving,
and is saved from sentimentality by its tough simplicity. Such
moments of decision are the dramatic backbone of Brecht's
plays, just as the portraying of decision is central to his style of
acting.

There is an opportunity for a magnificent moment of this
sort in *The Life of Galileo* (1947), but Brecht deliberately rejects it.
Instead of being shown Galileo himself in front of the Inquisi-
tion, we see the event through the eyes of his followers who
confidently expect him to refuse to recant. Brecht wants, in this
way, to emphasize the harm done to his contemporaries and to
posterity by Galileo's recantation. He nipped in the bud, Brecht
argues, the new spirit of free enquiry which was spreading to

the market place and which might have become a common pursuit; and, by making the scientist a servant of the state, he initiated the attitude which now makes possible the manufacture of the hydrogen bomb. 'Change the world, it needs it!' is a theme which runs through Brecht's plays. His Galileo is a man who had a chance to change the world and who failed to take it.

Galileo is Brecht's most fully argued play—the alien attitudes of the Church, for example, are admirably expressed—and it is more likely than any of the others to fulfil his aim and to send an audience out arguing on to the streets. Early in the play Galileo plagiarizes the Dutch invention of the telescope in order to make enough money to continue his research, an act of practical dishonesty which has Brecht's full approval. Knowing therefore that it enabled him to finish the Discorsi, one assumes that the recantation will be presented as a larger version of the same act, a reassessment of conventional honour similar to the soldier's strategic flight in The Horatii and the Curatii. And, in fact, in an early version of the play Brecht did show Galileo to be justified. He later changed his mind, partly because of Hiroshima, and in the final version Galileo condemns himself. He says that he recanted only from cowardice, when he was shown the instruments of torture, and that a man like himself can no longer be 'tolerated in the ranks of science'.

> He who does not know the truth is merely an idiot. But he who knows it and calls it a lie, is a criminal,[27]

he says. His disciple Andrea, overjoyed that the Discorsi have been finished, retorts: 'I cannot believe that your murderous analysis will be the last word.' And Brecht himself stands, as a playwright should, between the two of them with his comment:

> In spite of all, he is a hero—and in spite of all—he becomes a criminal.[28]

The doubt was Brecht's own. His own behaviour was always more cunning than idealistic: for example, he eagerly assured the Un-American Activities Committee that he had never had anything to do with Communism, and before finally settling in East Berlin he made sure that he had an Austrian passport and a Swiss bank account. His plays are full of similarly foxy characters: Mother Courage with her Song of Capitulation, Azdak who will do anything to save his skin, Matti in *Puntila and His Man Matti* (1940) and Galileo himself, on any but the central issue. As much as any of these characters, Brecht distrusted heroism and extremist positions, yet he was also fascinated by them. In his 'didactic' period he pressed characters to un-necessary extremes of self-sacrifice for the sake of the party. School-children watching *He Who Said Yes* commented that the boy's death could be avoided, so Brecht rewrote the ending for them and called the play *He Who Said No*. Yet only a few months later he was writing *The Measures Taken* in which once again, as Ronald Gray has pointed out,[29] the reasons for killing the young comrade are very briefly sketched in and seem hardly watertight. His death is eagerly assumed to be inevi-table, rather than sorrowfully proved so: it is Brecht, rather than the logic of his situation, who is forcing the extreme conclusion.

His attitude to the problem of moral challenges seems like that of a boy confronted with a high tree near his house. Sometimes he makes himself climb to the top; more frequently he points out the futility of such heroism and so rationalizes his desire to stay on the ground. The ideal solution would be to cut down the tree, with its challenge or temptation, and indeed this turns out to be Brecht's idea of Utopia. Andrea shouts at Galileo, immediately after his recantation:

Unhappy the land that has no heroes!

Galileo replies

No. Unhappy the land that is in need of heroes[30]

and Mother Courage echoes the same sentiment when she says that only incompetent generals require courage of their soldiers.

The temptation of goodness is terrible; and the world must be changed to make it unnecessary.

This is a long way from the orthodox Communist Utopia, in which Everyman's virtues are embarrassingly monumental, and it is not surprising that Brecht's plays have been almost totally neglected in Moscow while achieving fame in the West. Comparison with any party-line Communist play reveals how false it is to think of Brecht's work as being 'political' in the derogatory sense of 'propagandist'. Brecht states problems instead of offering solutions. Crying 'Change the world, it needs it!' he concentrates entirely on the world as it is—on why it should be changed, not how. Though his plays imply the possibility of a Utopia, however low-keyed and unheroic, they never give us a glimpse of it; and even when his setting is specifically that of modern Communism, as in *The Measures Taken*, he immediately goes to the awkward moral dilemma inherent in the situation. His work is political in the sense that it delves into the dilemmas of man, a political animal. But 'moral' remains a less confusing label for his real concern; or more precisely, perhaps, in John Willett's phrase, 'moral-social'.

12

Jean Giraudoux 1882–1944

IN A review of Giraudoux's first play, *Siegfried* (1928), Etienne Rey wrote:

> It is an enchantment to listen to this dialogue in which intelligence, sensitivity, all the resources of culture revel in the most ingenious exercises.[31]

Revelry in the most ingenious and cultured exercises was both the appeal and the limitation of Giraudoux's early plays. The hero of *Siegfried*, for example, is a French writer who loses his memory and identity during the First World War and who later becomes a leading German politician. He is several times compared to Oedipus. The analogy provides one or two very effective theatrical moments but adds nothing to the meaning of the play. It remains a brilliant and sophisticated piece of embroidery.

Amphitryon 38 (1929) is still in the same vein. Critics have claimed too much for it when they argue that it deals with such subjects as the proper relationship between man and God. Its limits are those of a witty comedy of intrigue and paradox, for which the subject of Jupiter's seduction of the virtuous Alcmena by taking on the appearance of her husband is ideally suited.

But within these limits some of Giraudoux's particular talents were already appearing. One of them was the quality of his imagination, which could seize and bring down into concrete terms of experience any flight of fantasy, as in Leda's description to an apprehensive Alcmena of what it was like to be seduced by Jupiter in the form of a swan. Another element very typical of the later Giraudoux was the gentle satire of human behaviour from the standpoint of fantasy—in this case Jupiter's instruction of Mercury in the weird and elaborate routine of human love-making.

Both these plays were immediate successes, but although Giraudoux greatly extended his range in his third play, *Judith* (1931), and wrote several scenes which far surpassed anything he had yet done, its first production was a dismal failure. This was perhaps understandable. It had aimed far higher than the others and it fell a little short of its mark, whereas they had been completely successful within their own limits.

Giraudoux's Judith is a complicated young girl whose personality undergoes a series of changes on the way to her biblical assignment in Holofernes' bed. At each point she believes that she is behaving with complete honesty, but events reveal in her attitude a series of conventional religious excesses which amount almost to cant: she has an excessive humility, then an excessive sense of purity, then an excessive pride in her God-sent mission, then an excessive desire to abase herself. Each of these is stripped from her, until, when she finally confronts Holofernes, she stands before him simply as a young woman; when she sleeps with him she does so because she wants to. The Judith-Holofernes battle, says Giraudoux, has been whittled down to its barest essentials, to an encounter between 'a brown body and a white body'. And when she kills him at the end of the night it is because the dawn can only bring the end of their love affair, not because the city needs saving.

From this point, this barest bedrock of honesty, the wrapping-up process begins. The triumphant Jewish chroniclers arrive, determined that Judith is a national heroine, a martyr who has in the most distressing circumstances sacrificed her self and her virginity for God and country—all the things, in fact, which she has discovered that she is not. This situation provides Giraudoux with some of his best scenes. No dramatist has been more aware than he of the literary weight and texture of language, and while the chroniclers stride around hymning her triumph with biblical solemnity, Judith quietly, calmly and in the clearest of simple images insists that she killed their enemy for love.

The high-priest Joachim and her uncle Paul then take her

aside and explain to her the political necessity for her to become a national figurehead. (This scene-behind-the-scenes, a confrontation of individuals trapped by the machinery of political necessity, anticipates much of French drama for the next fifteen years.) But Judith is adamant, until, suddenly, she sees an apparition of God in which he tells her that this is her chosen destiny. She accepts this, announces that she killed Holofernes for the good of the city and agrees to become the chief of the temple virgins who deal out punishment.

> Let the procession start . . . Judith the saint is ready

are her last words.

This miraculous *volte-face* must have been the main stumbling-block for the audience, because it throws into doubt the meaning of the whole play. To most people Judith's fate would seem a disaster and Giraudoux's ending therefore bitterly satirical. This girl, who has found a moment of honest love, now has to deny it for the sake of appearances and to start a joyless life that amounts almost to death. Yet, if that was the author's intention, Judith's defeat should surely have been contrived by the priests, not brought about by a miracle. For the miracle is presented as genuine and can come only as a bewildering shock, since religion has up to this point been inseparable from politics and since Holofernes' tent, which seems an ideal place to be, has been described as an area from which the gods are excluded.

Judith contained three elements which were to become typical of Giraudoux—ambiguity of meaning, a vivid simplicity of images, and drama rising from a struggle between eternal opposites. In this case it was between honesty and cant, between the ideal and the expedient. In his next play, *Intermezzo*, it would be between the magical and the mundane, in *Sodom and Gomorrah* between the male and the female, in *The Madwoman of Chaillot* between the natural and the commercial, in *Duel of Angels* between purity and compromise. The details of the contrast are different from play to play, but the form of it is always the same—a balance of extremes.

The ambiguity is particularly strong in *Intermezzo* (1933), the story of a young school-teacher, Isabelle, who falls in love with Death and with fantasy. She no longer teaches her class the set syllabus. One little girl, when asked by the Inspector what a tree is, answers:

> The tree is man's stationary brother. In its language assassins are known as lumberjacks, undertakers as charcoal-burners, and fleas as green woodpeckers.

The officials of the small town realize the danger of such a strange perspective and set about rescuing Isabelle from her illusions. They finally succeed when they convince her that there is also poetry in their conventional way of life. The Controller recites to her all the medieval names of the weights and measures used in his trade and everyone gathers round at the end to provide a chorus of all the small sounds of everyday life, a cacophony which eventually wins her over. So Isabelle becomes an adult. The Ghost who has haunted her says that he will be appearing to her daughter in fifteen years' time. Giraudoux, it is clear, sees this romanticism as an 'intermezzo' in every young girl's life.

A play is satisfactorily ambiguous when the playwright, and through him the spectators, feel an equally powerful sympathy for both sides of a struggle. Giraudoux is attracted both to Isabelle's view of life and to that of his little officials, but he fails to pass on this attraction. Isabelle's fantasy is pure whimsy and the small joys of life ('the lyricism of officialdom' is the phrase used by one of the characters) seem merely ridiculous. So *Intermezzo* has no positives of its own, and yet lacks the savagery of satire.

Tiger at the Gates (*La Guerre de Troie n'aura pas Lieu*, 1935) is probably Giraudoux's best play. Some of the themes of *Judith* reappear in it, but in a much less ambiguous form. Its tone is both lighter and stronger. From the very first line, Andromache's determined cry: 'There's not going to be a Trojan War, Cassandra!', one knows where Giraudoux's sympathies lie. The implications of Judith's fate were in doubt, but the Trojan War will undeniably be a disaster. Hector's attempts to prevent it are therefore consistently and straightforwardly admirable.

His efforts for peace are thwarted, as was Judith's honesty, by false ideas of heroism and of glory, and—a new element—by people's indifference. But in addition to being a biting satire, guying the sentimentally jingoistic old men, the effusive poet laureate who is determined to write a war-song, and so forth, the play is heightened by Giraudoux's remarkably concrete imagery. Here, as always, he turns every idea into colour, into solid details. Helen cares little whether or not she goes back to Greece. Giraudoux expresses this indifference through her claim that she always sees very vividly anything that is going to happen, but that her departure remains totally drab in her mind. Hector, trying to persuade her to leave, describes the scene for her:

> We are going to give you back to the Greeks at high noon, on the blinding sand, between the violet sea and the ochre-coloured wall. We shall all be in golden armour with red skirts; and my sisters, dressed in green and standing between my white stallion and Priam's black mare, will return you to the Greek ambassador, over whose silver helmet I can imagine tall purple plumes. You see that, I think?

'No, none of it. It is all quite sombre,' replies Helen. Later in the scene, when Hector has lost patience, he tells her curtly:

> You will go back on a grey sea under a grey sun. But we must have peace.[32]

The imagery works dramatically; it is not mere decoration, nor in itself the point of the scene, but something deeper—its idiom. In other words it is a theatrical metaphor.

The implications of *Tiger at the Gates* are clear, and the defeated hero is a pragmatist. 'Idealism' is a form of cant, and is claimed by Priam for himself and the other dotards who are infatuated with Helen. In *Electra* (1937) idealism is on the heroine's side; but, once again, it is not wholly admirable.

Electra is Giraudoux's most complicated play. The heroine's psychology is as complex as was Judith's, and Giraudoux's own attitude to her is ambivalent. She is in some ways made magnificent. She is a pure and rare creature of tragedy (Anouilh was to take over from Giraudoux, amongst other things, this concept of an élite of tragedy), who can retort to a conciliatory proposal of Aegisthus':

> You mock me, Aegisthus. Can you, who profess to know me, believe that I'm one of the breed to whom you can say 'Tell a lie, let others share it, and you'll have a prosperous fatherland: hide guilt and your country will be victorious.'? What is this poor fatherland that you're trying to slip in between the truth and us?

And yet Giraudoux stacks the odds in every possible way against her idealism, even changing the classical story for the purpose. In most versions of the story it is common knowledge that Aegisthus and Clytaemnestra are lovers, and the murderers of Agamemnon: in this Argos nobody but Electra suspects such a thing. Where Aegisthus is usually a rascal and the people of Argos are in a high state of disturbance, Aegisthus is here the excellent and kindly leader of a contented people. Thus it is not a question of Electra's preventing guilt being hidden—she specifically has to dig it up. And when she does so, disasters follow. Argos burns and hundreds of innocent people die. Electra says:

> I have my conscience, I have Orestes, I have justice, I have everything.

The Furies point out that she certainly has not her conscience, since she was tortured by guilt even before committing these crimes against her mother and stepfather, and now it will be worse; nor has she Orestes, because they are driving him away. Electra is left muttering: 'I have justice, I have everything.' And yet the play ends with dawn breaking—cold and cruel perhaps, but fresh too.

So *Electra* is neither a simple condemnation of blind, impractical, selfish idealism, nor an affirmation of it. Giraudoux was strongly attracted to idealism and yet repelled by its results. *Electra* is a testing of it. In *Tiger at the Gates* Giraudoux had been certain what he was against; now he was uncertain what he was for. The ambiguity of the earlier plays has grown deeper, but the despair is still tempered and made dramatic by irony and wit. Typical of the mood of *Electra* is the Gardener's challenge to the gods to prove themselves creatures of joy and love by *not* shouting out: 'Joy and love.' The ensuing silence is all the evidence he needs.

After this plunge into the depths of ambiguity and doubt, *Ondine* (1939) is a pleasantly superficial fairy-story. Its theme—that human society is unable to contain this pure, supernatural creature, Ondine, whose simplicity and honesty play havoc with the conventions of life at the royal court—has all the Giraudoux preoccupations, but they are food for delight and fantasy rather than for anything more serious. *Sodom and Gomorrah* (1943) uses the threat of the end of the world as a pretext for a brilliant discussion of the human couple, the contrast of extremes being, this time, the essentially romantic female and the essentially prosaic male. Giraudoux's inventiveness is as lively as ever, but the play suffers from the lack of a plot and becomes a series of talkative tableaux. *The Madwoman of Chaillot* (1943) satirizes capitalist entrepreneurs effectively, though somewhat obviously, and sets against them the naïve spontaneity of a mad old woman and her friends. This time, unlike *Intermezzo*, there is nothing whatever to be said in favour of the earthbound characters. But there is still far too little to be said for the opposite side; too much of the madwoman's natural wisdom is, once again, just whimsy. Meanwhile, in a very slight little play, *The Apollo of Bellac* (1942), Giraudoux had written the simplest statement of his sorrow over the place of honesty in the world. The heroine, Agnes, finds that all doors will open to her if she merely says to every man, regardless of how hideous he may be, 'How beautiful you are!'

With a neatness dear to the heart of a critic, Giraudoux brought all the threads of his drama together in his last play,

Duel of Angels (*Pour Lucrèce*, 1944). Ibsen had done the same in *When We Dead Awaken*; but whereas that has merit only as a key to the rest of his work, *Duel of Angels* is also, in itself, an excellent play.

Lucile Blanchard, the Lucretia of the story, is very pure and devastatingly honest. She also has a magical ability to recognize dishonesty in others—an adulteress to her is a woman with insects crawling all over her face—and she is too ingenuous to hide her reactions to these insights. Soon apparently happy marriages are breaking up simply because Lucile has snubbed the wife. The whole fabric of small-town life begins to crumble. To protect it from this blast of honesty, Paola, a woman of the world and an adulteress recently recognized as such by Lucile, plays a trick on her. She drugs Lucile and arranges evidence which will make her think she has been raped in her sleep by Marcellus, a local Don Juan. But to Lucile the rape constitutes a marriage, the only relationship in which she can imagine herself; she can therefore become free to return to her real husband only if Marcellus is dead. As a result of this extreme reaction Marcellus is challenged to a duel and is killed, but the events also lead to the collapse of Lucile's own marriage. A more mature, or a more cynical, reaction would have avoided these disasters. It makes no difference to Lucile when she discovers that she has not even, in reality, been defiled. Like Anouilh's Antigone, in despair over the world which she has now discovered, she commits suicide.

In this story Purity has revealed the world in its worst colours and has then died in horror at the sight. It was Lucile herself who started the ball rolling: if her penetrating gaze had not destroyed the comfortable surface of conventional life, all would have been well. Paola, in taking action against her, was merely trying to save the town from her searing honesty, just as Aegisthus tried to save Argos from Electra's. Both these heroines cause a great deal of 'harm', in the normal sense of the word, but Electra's achievements are accorded somewhat ironical praise. With Lucile, the ambiguity disappears. She dies because she cannot compromise, but she herself admits that she has been wrong.

Armand: Wrong to be true to yourself?

Lucile: To have had so much pride. Why should I have told
    Marcellus I was his wife? To have called it a marriage,
    instead of quite simply a great misfortune. Why wasn't I
    content to be the dishonoured wife with a loving,
    unhappy husband?[33]

Purity and idealism are at last in this play revealed as the
alternatives to maturity, confirming the hint in *Intermezzo* where
the Ghost warns that he will be appearing to Isabelle's daughter
in fifteen years' time. Paola is not a villainess; merely the mature
woman who has come to terms with the world. Lucile's death
is, in a sense, her refusal to grow up, refusal to learn to live with
'great misfortunes'. After a lifetime of struggle between the
opposites, Giraudoux has come down on the side of the world.
Duel of Angels is his regretful epitaph to purity. But, characteristically, the play in which he finally casts judgement against
purity is still dedicated to it, as the original French title implied.
Pour Lucrèce. For Lucretia.

    That he should come down on the side of the world was
always implicit in Giraudoux's work, because his peculiar talent
was to use fantasy to illuminate fact. Both in theme and style
this was so. Giraudoux has been much praised for his language,
for the rich and bright perfection of some of his speeches, and
it is no accident that Christopher Fry chose to translate his
plays and Anouilh's. But whereas metaphor sometimes seems
an end in itself in Fry's own plays (directing the audience's
attention to the speech, to art), it is always for Giraudoux the
means, directing attention to the fact, to life. In the best of
Giraudoux a speech can seem to be pure fantasy until it suddenly does a *volte-face* and proves to have been purified fact. In
Sodom and Gomorrah God will destroy the world unless he can find
one happy couple. John and Lia are put up by their neighbours
as candidates, but they soon have a violent quarrel. Someone
suggests that if they quickly strike up a pose of reconciliation
and affection all may yet be well. Lia reacts very strongly
against this:

So did God look away immediately after the last time we kissed? And will He look back at the precise moment when we kiss and make up? Without having seen anything in between? If so, Man can indulge in every conceivable indiscretion in between the glances of God . . . Is God the Father a mother?

This is an observation, not on God, but on mothers.

13

Jean Anouilh 1910–

THERE would be every reason for saying that the mantle of Giraudoux fell upon the shoulders of Jean Anouilh, a much younger man, were it not that Anouilh's first play, *The Ermine* (1931), appeared only three years after Giraudoux's. Like Giraudoux's, Anouilh's early plays were full of the spirit of playing with the theatre, but there was already a difference in the manner of the playing, a difference that was to grow greater in the later plays of the two men. Giraudoux's had been sophisticated playing, full of classical allusions. Anouilh's was much more purely theatrical. His third play, *The Thieves' Carnival* (1933), is a full-scale theatrical *jeu d'esprit*, using all the tricks of vaudeville and charade. It is a complete repertoire for a theatre magician, and foreshadows a play like *Time Remembered* (*Léocadia*, 1939), self-contained and self-inspiring in its own cocoon of fantasy: it equally makes unthinkable the idea of a future *Tiger at the Gates*, which drops classical allusions like Japanese flower-pills into water.

Anouilh's first considerable play was *The Wild One* (*La Sauvage*, 1935). It was to be the first of the five plays which are the centre and summit of his achievement—the other four being *Point of Departure* (1941), *Antigone* (1942), *Romeo and Jeannette* (1945) and *Medea* (1946). These five plays explore Anouilh's ideas of love and mere comfort, idealism and expediency, caring and not caring, happiness, guilt, life. They do not develop any common theme. They are linked merely by their shared values and doubts.

The Wild One is a young girl called Thérèse, whose background is sordid. She plays the violin in her father's small dance band and is surrounded by jealousies, lust and constant squabbles over money. But a rich young man, Florent, wants to marry her. This is her chance to break away from the sordid into a world where money is unimportant because it is taken for granted—her chance to be *happy*, a key word in Anouilh's canon. She moves into his world and is, for a while, happy; but she finds that the price of this happiness is spiritual death, a total separation from the real and suffering world outside. Her fiancé's relations are happy because they have never noticed unhappiness. She brings her father to stay at the big house in the perverse hope that his boorishness will shock her fiancé into throwing them out, but she comes up against the liberal's trump card: Florent is merely amused. She feels a surge of relief when Gosta, a member of the band who is passionately though unsuccessfully in love with her, bursts into the house threatening to shoot Florent. She decides that she must go back to the world where people can feel so strongly. The paradox of her attitude to happiness, and of Anouilh's, is expressed when she describes to her father the sort of happiness she wants:

> Thérèse: The happiness of having reached the depth of one's misery. You don't know it, you others, but at the very extreme of despair there is a bright strip where one is almost happy.
> Father: Strange sort of happiness.
> Thérèse: Yes, Father, a strange sort of happiness and one which has nothing in common with your sort. A dirty shameful happiness.

Then, a line or two later, she breaks down in a panic and cries:

> No. I want to be happy the way everyone else is.

In these lines Anouilh is already (in 1935) anticipating something of Sartre's existentialism in drama; for Sartre also, 'life begins on the far side of despair'. For both writers it is detachment that is death. And in Thérèse's scornful 'you others' and 'your sort of happiness' one has the concept of a Nietzschean élite of tragedy, a concept which runs through all these five plays and which was shared also by Giraudoux. In both dramatists *race* is the French word most commonly used in this context; the creatures of tragedy are presented as a separate breed—a modern version, perhaps, of the classical, pre-bourgeois tradition, by which royalty and nobility were the only proper victims of tragedy. In Anouilh's world the unhappy young heroes and heroines are capable of love and idealism, while the happy rest of the world merely eats and belches, copulates and sleeps. And this 'rest of the world' is usually represented by parents or nurses. As with Giraudoux, idealism is the antithesis of growing up.

This concept puts love into the realm of magic, and it is at its most purely magical in *Point of Departure* (*Eurydice*, 1941). Once again the play is set in the milieu of second-rate travelling entertainers and Orpheus's harp-playing father differs little from Thérèse's. Orpheus and Eurydice fall for each other instantly, the phrase 'at first sight' being turned directly into action on the stage. Their happiness together in a dingy hotel room is immediate, perfect and short-lived. It is broken when the sordid and unmeant affairs from Eurydice's past intrude on it. She dies and, as in the legend, is given back to Orpheus on one condition, that he does not look at her until the morning. His jealousy makes him look at her—to see whether even now she is telling him the whole truth about her earlier love-life— and she dies again. At the end of the play he too dies and rejoins her. So the rose of ideal love had the worm of worldliness even inside itself; it is possible only for a moment in life, or else after death. As the nurse said in *Duel of Angels*: 'Purity is not for this world, but every ten years we get a gleam of it.'

Taken by itself, this plot would be intolerably whimsical. It is saved by its wordly setting. What determines Orpheus to die at the end is not so much his love for Eurydice as his father's attempts to persuade him to live. The real climax of the play is not the parting of the lovers: it is this fat old man's lengthy eulogy on the pleasures of women, food and cigars. The old man is satirized, but his attitude is not rejected out of hand, even though it horrifies the pure Orpheus. He is certainly no mere cipher to offset the ideal lovers. The battle between the world and the ideal is less abstract in Anouilh than in Giraudoux, but no less undecided.

The world was on trial in *Point of Departure*; in *Antigone* (1942) the searchlight is turned on to the ideal, and it emerges from the test none too well. Antigone's idealistic obstinacy undergoes many changes before she finally dies. At first it seems a simple act of duty towards a much-wronged brother. Creon explains to her all the practical reasons of government why Polyneices must be made a scapegoat, but these naturally fail to convince her—any purely 'practical' reason is a bad reason to one of her breed. But then Creon tells her how villainous both her brothers were (they tried to have their father murdered) and admits that he does not even know whether the body rotting in the open is Eteocles or Polyneices. They were both so mangled in a cavalry charge as to be unidentifiable, but all that Creon needed was one body left out on the sand. This piece of news so disillusions Antigone that she agrees to give up her protest and to live—simply because there is nothing worth dying for. But then Creon goes too far. He describes the happiness she will have in later life, the happiness of the small pleasures of the world. 'Your filthy happiness!' is Antigone's reaction, and once more she determines to make her stand and die—there is nothing worth living for either. In prison she loses her last shred of confidence and finally dies, like Giraudoux's Lucile in the very similar *Duel of Angels*, convinced that Creon was right, and terrified of a pointless death. Her death results in two others, both equally pointless. Haemon, her fiancé and Creon's son, spits in his father's face over her dead body and stabs himself. His mother, Creon's wife Eurydice, has been living for years a quiet life of monotony, just knitting for the poor. When she hears the news of Haemon's death she calmly finishes her row, sets aside her needles, walks into her bathroom and cuts her throat. A pointless life has been exchanged for a pointless death—such would seem to be the implication. Creon goes in to a council meeting. Life must go on.

Yet Creon is not presented as being any more 'right' than Antigone. He has merely suffered the misfortune of growing up; he has taken on responsibility, and with it the duty of saying 'yes' to any necessary expedient, where Antigone still has the right to say 'no'. But Creon is a reluctant utilitarian: he did not want this responsibility, and part of him envies Antigone, remembering the time when he was like her. He is middle age, the world—she is youth, idealism. Both are essential and both incomplete, both right and both wrong. When the play opened in Paris in 1942 some people took it as a magnificent resistance play, others as a blatant justification of collaboration. The confusion is understandable—it is the author's own. It is the creative doubt and agony behind all his best plays.

Romeo and Jeannette (1945) returns to the theme of *Point of Departure*. Love is still a matter of magic. Frederick is engaged to a straightforward, upright and beautiful girl, Julia. When she takes him to meet her family, he instantly falls for her wild sister, Jeannette, but in their brief affair he is shocked by the details of her past, and he has too much sense of responsibility (he is too nearly grown-up) to accept her way of life. He returns to Julia. To spite him, Jeannette marries a rich old neighbour but leaves the wedding festivities to taunt him in her magnificent white dress. Almost without noticing it (they hold a kiss in the path of the rising tide) they commit suicide together. The play is not particularly successful, though it has some superb scenes. The best of all typifies Anouilh's conception of rare creatures of romance and tragedy who are set apart from the rest of the world. While Frederick and Jeannette go through their first magical love-scene (quiet, even remote, lines, spoken far apart on a slowly darkening stage), the rest of the family get on with the housework.

Julia represents the normal idea of romance and purity—the fiancée who will be a virgin bride in white. Jeannette, Anouilh's romantic ideal, another Thérèse, another Eurydice, is something much more wild and *rive gauche*. Her white wedding dress for the rich old neighbour was an empty mockery, like the wedding itself. She offers herself to Frederick 'without a bouquet, without a veil, with no innocence and no little children to hold a train . . . a bride all in black'—and, in Anouilh's romantic world, the only sort of bride for love.

There was to be only one more bride in black—Medea. *Medea* (1946) is the culmination of these five plays and of Anouilh's struggle of opposites. Although only a one-act play, it contains all his themes. It has the élite for whom love is

pure and hate is pure, and compromise the only evil. It has
the ordinary people turning with relief from Medea's tragedy
back to their glass of wine in the sun. And it has the heroine's
desire for, and fear of, happiness: Medea admits that she would
like to be happy, but says that happiness without superficiality
is impossible in this world. All this makes it the essence of these
five plays, but another reason makes it also their climax. For the
first time, one of 'us' is trying to join 'them'; a member of the
élite is trying to find a place in the world.

This turncoat is Jason. He is married to a bride in black,
Medea, but he now wants to marry Creon's daughter; and it
will be a magnificent white wedding. In the central scene of the
play, when Medea and Jason confront each other, he explains
to her that he is too tired not to compromise, too tired to
continue in her way of life. He wants only happiness and peace.

> Jason: Go your own way. Turn in circles, lacerate yourself,
> mistrust everything, insult, kill, refuse all that isn't 'you'.
> But I stop here. I'm content with things as they are. I
> accept appearances as rigidly and as fully as I once
> rejected them with you. And if I still have to fight, it's for
> them that I'll be fighting now, humbly and with my back
> to the ridiculous wall which I will have built with my
> own hands between the absurd empty universe and
> myself.
>
> *(he pauses)*
> And surely that, when you come to the point, that and
> nothing else is the meaning of becoming a man.
> Medea: You can be sure of that, Jason. You are a man now.

Jason has grown up. Again, as so often in Anouilh, there are
traces of existentialism in this—there is even Camus's precise
use of the word 'absurd'—but they are misleading. Anouilh's
philosophy is romantic and vague, and to formulate it leads to
strange conclusions. For example, Antigone and Medea are
clearly on the same side of the fence, yet in another sense Medea
is more like Creon. He is committed to saying 'yes' to the needs
of his city, and she describes herself as being bound to say 'yes'

to whatever her love for Jason demands—even to murder. Sartre's existentialism, on the other hand, is a consistent and practical philosophy. The difference is clearest in the matter of 'becoming a man'. For Sartre commitment is becoming a man is life. For Anouilh acceptance is becoming a man is death.

Meanwhile, faced by Jason's growing up (he refers to their relationship as having been like 'two brothers'), Medea fights harder than any other Anouilh heroine to preserve the high purity of her romantic position. The facts about the corpse rotting in the sand had deflated Antigone, but Medea can rise above mere facts. When the nurse remarks that Jason's new wedding is no very great tragedy, since for some time Medea and he have even preferred to sleep separately, Medea kicks at her and snaps: 'You know too much. Get back to your sweeping with the rest of your kind.'

So, in her extremity, Medea makes the most purely and highly arrogant stand for idealism (of a kind), while Jason, like all new converts, puts the best possible case for compromise. Through Antigone's doubts and Creon's regrets, *Antigone* had stressed the negative aspects of both sides: it is Anouilh's most nihilistic play. *Medea*, stressing the positives, is his fiercest and his best. It is presumably because it is only in one act that it is so little known.

In culminating the theme of opposites *Medea* was for Anouilh what *Duel of Angels* had been for Giraudoux. But, unlike *Duel of Angels*, it was not Anouilh's last play. He had to move on with Jason into 'grown-up' love, and his next play, *Ardèle* (1948), was the harsh result. Far from being magical, love is now explained in the most cynical of terms. One person loves another, the play argues, because he can see a reflection of himself in the loved one. So the relationship is not a giving of oneself, as it is normally explained, but a taking of oneself. When the loved one changes a little, the lover can no longer see a reflection of himself. He therefore moves on—and hence so many broken affairs. It is a logical conclusion of this that the two happiest and most faithful lovers in *Ardèle* are a pair of hunchbacks. For them the image is defined in more detail than for others; and, of course, alternative mirrors are harder to come by. So much for love, says Anouilh: so much for Anouilh is more likely to be the audience's reaction. For, though *Ardèle* has some very funny scenes, it is too exclusively a hotch-potch of disgust.

Up to this point Anouilh had called his plays either *Pièces Roses* or *Pièces Noires*. *Ardèle* was the first of a series published as *Pièces Grinçantes*—harsh plays, literally 'grating'—and he has called two more recent volumes *Pièces Brillantes* and *Pièces Costumées*. These three labels, grating, brilliant and costumed, define well the limitations of Anouilh's plays since *Medea*. They veer between cynicism, empty subtlety and the spectacular. The old themes recur, but they are hollow, unfelt. In *Colombe* (1950) the innocent young heroine changes into a callous woman of the world without so much as noticing it. In *The Rehearsal* (1951) cynical aristocrats take pleasure in ruining an apparently happy love affair by a series of well-contrived lies. In *The Lark* (1952) Joan of Arc capitulates, like Antigone, until Warwick tells her of happiness and adult life, when she becomes determined to die; but the play seems geared to theatrical effects and to spectacular scenes. (As for the 'lark' theme, it is Shaw's Joan who is more lark-like, taking back her confession when she hears that she will be caged.) The same criticism goes for the much-praised but very superficial *Becket* (1959), a study of Henry II and Thomas Becket which is more pageant than tragedy.

A character in Giraudoux's *Sodom and Gomorrah* is described by another as speaking 'a beautiful language, without abstract words and without adjectives'. This was true of Giraudoux himself and it is true of Anouilh. Wherever possible they both turn ideas into concrete images. This, together with his great sense of theatre, saves Anouilh's recent plays from being merely mediocre—but not from being, by his own standards, very disappointing.

14

Jean-Paul Sartre 1905–

AFTER the doubts of Giraudoux and Anouilh, the certainty of Sartre. His first play, *The Flies* (1943), specifically shows a man growing from a position of vague liberal detachment to one of commitment, from inaction to action—the existentialist ideal. When Orestes first arrives in Argos with his tutor he can overlook the suffering of the people and he spends his energies discussing the niceties of the Doric pillars. By the end of the play he has murdered Clytaemnestra and Aegisthus and, most important, has insisted on taking full personal responsibility for his action. By so doing he rescues the people of Argos from their crippling sense of communal guilt for the death of Agamemnon, a state in which Aegisthus and Zeus, their temporal and spiritual rulers, have found it politic to keep them.

The play could be used as a manual of Sartrian existentialism. Sartre's main tenet is that 'existence precedes essence'. This means that there is no such thing as 'human nature', no Platonic form of mankind for each individual to be measured against. Each man is a blank slate on which he will, by his actions, come to define his own being. Orestes at the beginning of *The Flies* was therefore non-existent as a person. He had done nothing, he had committed himself to nothing, he belonged nowhere. He constantly refers to himself at this stage as being light, floating, disembodied. It is his definitive act of murder which gives him weight and turns him into a man. This in itself makes it essential that he should not then disown his action. Zeus, still hoping to restore the *status quo* and to keep the people of Argos in subservience, pleads with him to repent. But Orestes knows the power, even against the gods, of a free human being. He meant his action, even though the performance of it was intensely painful; and he would, if necessary,

repeat it.   Zeus is defeated. The flies which have been plaguing
Argos swarm around Orestes, and like the Pied Piper of Hamelin
he leads them away from the city.

The ideological content is not, of course, what makes *The
Flies* a good play. Its merit is that the classical story fits Sartre's
meaning as snugly as if he had invented it, and that the details
of his theme are all successfully dramatized. The plague of flies,
for example, besides being an effective version of the Furies (an
idea probably taken from Giraudoux, who in his *Electra* compares
the Eumenides to flies), is also an apt symbol for the festering
guilt in Argos. Again, Orestes needs to be sure, before taking the
fatal step, that no less violent solution is possible. He finds out
in an admirable scene in which Electra tries to win the people of
Argos back to life by appearing at the great annual ceremony of
repentance in a dazzling white dress and dancing through the
crowd. She almost succeeds—so much so that Zeus has to use a
minor miracle to bring the crowd to heel again. (Sartre in this
play allows God the possibility of existence but merely stresses
his unimportance to the free human being.)

His next piece, *No Exit* (*Huis Clos*, 1944), may well be a convincing version of life after death, but it has very little relevance
to life before it. Three recently dead people are shut up together
for eternity. Ines is a Lesbian: she desires Estelle, a nym-
phomaniac who desires Garcin, the only male. But his one
desire is to be convinced that the manner of his death does not
prove him a coward. Since Estelle will tell him anything for a
caress, he has to rely on Ines. The vicious circle of personal
relationships is complete. 'Hell,' concludes Garcin, 'is other
people,' and it is on this apparently profound statement that the
play's reputation for seriousness seems to rest. Yet Ines, Estelle
and Garcin can hardly claim to be a fair sample of 'other
people'—it would certainly require great ingenuity to devise
another such 'hellish' trio. Even apart from their excessively
neat emotional interdependence now, their separate lives on
earth glowed brightly with murder, suicide and sadism. The
truth is that the meaning of *No Exit* is minimal. It is a Grand
Guignol idea which is brilliantly executed—for certainly Sartre
squeezes the last vivid drop of poison from his trio. Hades, as a

setting, has one indispensable advantage. None of them can leave it.

Sartre's subsequent plays all failed, like *No Exit*, to reach the standard of *The Flies*. *The Respectful Prostitute* (1944) is a melodrama on the theme of false respect. The Louisiana prostitute resists the force brought to bear on her to give false witness against a negro, but succumbs to the patriotic arguments that Uncle Sam needs the all-American white boy who has in fact committed the crime, and to the sentimental picture of the boy's mother weeping by herself in the big house. In the same way an innocent negro cannot bring himself to fire in self-defence on a lynch-crazy white man, simply because of his deep-seated respect for the colour of his skin. The play has been dismissed as grossly exaggerated. But the reason for this impression is not so much that Sartre has distorted the white Southern attitudes, as that, by providing too pat a plot, he has swamped his meaning in melodrama.

Men Without Shadows (*Morts sans Sepultures*, 1946) is a justifiably gruesome play about resistance workers being tortured for information by the Pétainists. It contains, like Camus's resistance plays, the slow death of personality and of love; and it forces its battered heroes to the extreme sacrifice of choosing not to die but to stagger back into the painful battle outside. Such violent subject-matter contains its own, somewhat limited, drama, but in Sartre's next play, *Crime Passionel* (*Les Mains Sales*, 1948), the dramatic interest seems smeared on to the surface like icing. The comedy is mechanically efficient, and the thrills depend on the oldest of melodramatic tricks: at least four times a character enters coincidentally at a crucial moment. In the story, which takes the form of one long flash-back, a resistance worker is on trial. He was ordered to carry out a political assassination, but failed to achieve his mission until he came across the victim kissing his wife. Was the murder a *crime passionel* or merely brilliantly disguised as such by a dedicated political assassin? The young man, while in prison, has convinced himself that it was the latter: such an action defines him, in existentialist terms, as the person whom he desires to be. As he unfolds his story to another resistance worker, who must judge whether they can use him again or must shoot him as a bad security risk, it becomes clear that he is a hopelessly weak man who fired the bullet purely on impulse. The ironical twist comes when his judge announces that he need not be shot. The reason is that policy has changed: the victim is now revered as a martyr; and his assassin can be used again provided he will change his name and keep his mouth shut. This Jean refuses to do, thus at last, in the Sartrian sense, 'becoming a man'. If he denies his action, he denies himself. He chooses to be shot.

All these plays were written within five years. In the next ten years Sartre produced only two more, neither of them successful. *Lucifer and the Lord* (*Le Diable et le Bon Dieu*, 1951) is a rambling great piece which is swamped by its philosophizing. It shows Goetz, a sixteenth-century buccaneering nobleman, in total dedication first to Evil and then, after a bet, to Good. In neither is he particularly successful. His real achievement begins only when he becomes prepared, like Orestes, to commit evil actions towards a good end. For the existentialist the vital act must be a practical one. Five years later came *Nekrassov* (1956), a satirical farce on an undergraduate level about Western politics and journalism.

Sartre's career as a playwright seemed to have ended, and retrospectively his achievement seemed not very high. A first play, in which form and content had merged perfectly to fulfil a clear-cut but fairly limited objective, had been followed by six others which ranged from the melodramatic to the undramatic and in which the meaning was often awkwardly separate from the drama. And on re-reading these plays one becomes aware of a frequent indulgence in gore. The descriptions of Clytaemnestra's death, of the lynching of a negro, or of Goetz's brother being eaten by wolves, are all unnecessarily gruesome in their context. Much of *Men without Shadows* is spent in interpreting the details of the torture in the room below from the stray sounds that break through, and Estelle kills her baby in *No Exit* by tying it to a large stone and throwing it off an hotel balcony into a lake. One knows Sartre's horror of torture from his writings about Algeria, but in art it is sometimes difficult to distinguish an author's horror from fascination. Certainly there are countless moments in his plays when audiences will either be pointlessly shocked or secretly thrilled—neither of them an admirable effect.

However, in 1959, Sartre redeemed his early promise in *Altona* (*Les Séquestrés d'Altona*), a massive, almost Gothic play, a dense tangle of guilt and possessiveness. This guilt has its most obsessive expression in the ravings of Frantz Gerlach, a wartime officer in the German army who since 1946 has shut himself away in the attic of his family home. Up there, surrounded by empty champagne bottles and oyster shells, he records on tape a crazy defence-cum-indictment of the twentieth century before an imagined jury of thirtieth-century crabs.

The guilt becomes specific when Frantz, after giving several evasive reasons for his self-imposed exile from the world, finally admits that in the war he tortured prisoners. Having confessed this, he wants his father to admit to a share of the responsibility. Gerlach is Germany's leading shipbuilder, and an industrial Vicar of Bray. He worked with Hitler, then with the Allies, then with Adenauer, and is now more prosperous than ever. Gerlach is responsible for Frantz's actions because he brought him up to admire the ruthless standards of materialism and at the same time always pulled strings to get the boy out of trouble. Once father and son have each admitted their responsibility to the other, they commit suicide together. Frantz's harsh sister, Leni, climbs the stairs to take his place in the attic: the net of responsibility widens. It spreads outwards to include all Germany, and, by implication, France and Algeria and wherever else the cap fits. It is presumably no accident that out of all the possible German names the central character should be called Frantz.

This criss-cross mesh of guilt is set in a tangled emotional plot which is almost as melodramatic as that of *No Exit*. But this time it suits the theme. The violent sexual drama, which includes incest, is in keeping with the festering of suppressed guilt, and the sheer force of the antagonism between the characters succeeds in breathing life into the dry intellectual aphorisms and paradoxes in which they express themselves. Sartre relies for the necessary passion on his cast; and good actors, given such explosive situations, can provide it. His own language has never been passionate. He is the opposite of King Claudius. His thoughts fly up, his words remain below.

In his previous plays Sartre's thought and his dramatic skill appear to have joined forces only a moment or two before he started writing. In *Altona* the two were hand in hand from some much earlier and murkier stage in the process of creation, and for the first time the thought itself seems tortured. It writhes with the drama.

15

T. S. Eliot 1888–1965

ELIOT sees our society as being in a state of comfortable and obstinate hibernation, a state resembling death. But winter must change to spring, the dead roots must shoot green again. The process of returning to life, like thawing out after frostbite, is painful. 'April is the cruellest month.' This image, and many others like it, first became familiar in Eliot's poetry. They continue throughout his plays.

Eliot had been publishing critical essays on poetic drama, and on the Jacobean dramatists in particular, for fifteen years before he himself wrote a full-length play. In 1935 he was commissioned to write a drama or pageant for the Canterbury Festival. It was to be performed in the cathedral and *Murder in the Cathedral* was the apt and excellent result.

It is the story both of Thomas Becket and of the people of Canterbury—the man and his society inextricably intertwined. Thomas is kept from a martyr's death by his fear of that sin which to saints is the most insidious of all, Pride; but he comes to accept his glorious fate and to 'lose his will in the will of God' when he sees how much the citizens of Canterbury need the strength and sense of purpose which his stand and death will bring them.

The seven years of his absence have been spiritually lean years for them. They themselves, true Eliot creatures, resist this return to life which Becket seems to promise them, this 'bitter spring'. They have taken refuge in the small pleasures of their everyday lives, on which Eliot dwells as frequently and as warmly as Anouilh, and they prefer to cower away from any challenge or danger. But by the end of the play they have moved to a position of responsibility and of involvement in the world.

We acknowledge
That the sin of the world is upon our heads; that the blood
            of the martyrs and the agony of the saints
Is upon our heads.

So Eliot's Canterbury chorus has followed the same path as
Aeschylus's chorus in the *Agamemnon*, which changes during the
play from dithering detachment to open opposition to Aegisthus. The awakening which follows most great tragedy is theirs.

The chief excellence of *Murder in the Cathedral* is its purity: it is
held together, not by its plot, which is virtually non-existent,
but by its theme. It is about the temptation and martyrdom of
Thomas and the awakening of the people of Canterbury; and,
without stepping aside for dramatic effects or light relief, it
relentlessly develops these twin themes. The only flaw in this
purity is the speeches of self-justification by the assassin Knights
near the end of the play, in which Eliot mistakenly gives their
arguments too much topicality. They produce all the routine
totalitarian rationalizations and so topple the play temporarily
into satire.

In *Murder in the Cathedral* Eliot admirably fulfilled his own
demands for poetic drama. The chief of these was that the
poetry should be a subtle regulator of mood, and here Eliot
succeeds fully (see pages 61–2). The poetry is the life-blood of the
play: the ideas, which are, in the main, abstract, are given
dramatic life purely by Eliot's concrete and vivid images. It is the
highest tribute to a poetic drama to say, as one can of *Murder in
the Cathedral*, that it is both intensely dramatic and inconceivable
in prose.

Yet he himself considered the play a 'dead end'. This was
partly because it was a religious festival play, and therefore
could incorporate a chorus more easily than other plays, but his
main reason was a conviction that significant drama should have
a modern setting—a restrictive fallacy which has followed in the
wake of Naturalism. Eliot therefore developed in his later plays
the weakest part of *Murder in the Cathedral*, the modernity of the
Knights, and dropped its greatest strength—the bright images
of poetry. Had he instead used his poetry as a medium for

plays with modern themes but distant settings (either in time or place), then *Murder in the Cathedral* might, after all, have heralded a new age of poetic drama. He would probably have had to do without the Greek type of chorus; but it is in no way indispensable to poetic drama, and he has in any case gradually had to eliminate it from his modern domestic plays.

The Family Reunion (1939), then, was the first step in the wrong direction. It is based very loosely on the Orestes story, the main similarity being that Harry Monchensey shares with his classical archetype the attentions of the Eumenides. They haunt him because he thinks he has pushed his wife overboard on a liner. He returns to his home, an English country house, hoping to find peace there but he finds none until he acquires the courage to face the Furies—to accept despair and guilt and to move beyond them towards self-fulfilment. He is given strength to do this by discovering that his father had murderous thoughts towards his mother while she was carrying him in her womb; i.e. he finds that sin is 'original' rather than purely personal. This realization that he is not alone, not unique, and that his sense of guilt is therefore not a mere sickness in himself but a part of life, is similar to Thomas's strength-giving discovery that the people of Canterbury depend on him. Thomas became a martyr; Harry leaves home again to become a missionary.

Judged by the highest standards, the play is unsuccessful; it is too much a tangle of awkward symbolic cross-references. This is the inevitable result of trying to write by means of poetic images and analogies in a naturalistic setting. At one point Dr Warburton mentions quite fortuitously that a patient of his was a murderer who had cancer. Harry develops from this an analogy, implicit to the audience but unnoticed by the other characters, between cancer and his own gnawing sense of guilt. At the end of it the doctor says:

> Well, let's not talk of such matters. How did we get on to the subject of cancer? I really don't know.

This abject apology is forced on Eliot purely by his naturalistic framework.

Part of Eliot's object in squeezing his poetic drama into the
modern drawing-room was to reach a wider public by working
inside the conventions of the commercial theatre, but he also
contrived to use the setting to his own ends. In fact the most
satisfactory symbol in The Family Reunion is in the very contrast
between the meaning of the play and its surface form. Just as the
citizens of Canterbury were prevented from moving into a new
life by their fondness for their small everyday pleasures, so the
surface trappings of bourgeois existence, on which domestic
comedy thrives, are what keep Eliot's new characters from
seeing below the surface into a deeper reality. He can at times
use this contrast to good dramatic effect. When disaster seems
to threaten, Harry's aunt, Ivy, turns away with:

> We must carry on as if nothing had happened,
> And have the cake and presents,

and at the end of the play Charles, an old man who has to his
surprise been disturbed by the revelations, expresses the
contrast in:

> I felt safe enough;
> And now I don't feel safe. As if the earth
>   should open
> Right to the centre, as I was about to cross
>   Pall Mall.

The concrete shock of 'cake and presents' and 'Pall Mall' is an
excellent use of the contrast between Eliot's convention and his
material, but the convention at other times runs away with him.
At one point a character says: 'I should have been helping Lady
Bumpus, at the Vicar's American tea.' This is intended to
suggest the triviality of the woman's life, but the line gets a
laugh in the theatre for all the reasons which contribute to the
success of run-of-the-mill drawing-room comedies—the amusing society name, the Vicar, even the mere idea of Americans
and of their having tea. It therefore detracts severely from
Eliot's play, and there are plenty of similar lines scattered

F

through it to bring the drama down from any heights it may be climbing to. In its worst aspect the drawing-room does for *The Family Reunion* what the Knights did for *Murder in the Cathedral*. Eliot 'will not need Pipit in heaven'. He should have done without her in the theatre too.

The Cocktail Party (1949) takes the trend further. There is less mystery in it than in *The Family Reunion*, and less poetry. A group of three people, referred to as the Guardians, concern themselves with the spiritual welfare of a married couple, Edward and Lavinia Chamberlayne, and of a girl in her twenties, Celia Coplestone. One of the three behaves as something between a psychiatrist and a confessor to these people and he succeeds by the end of the play in making them face themselves honestly, and so move on towards their own particular self-fulfilment. In the case of the Chamberlaynes this merely involves their working together to mend their marriage and to give better cocktail-parties, but Celia is a special case. Like Harry Monchensey, she is racked by a sense of guilt. This incapacitates her because she has grown up in the modern liberal atmosphere, so much hated by Eliot, in which

> anything wrong, from our point of view,
> Was either bad form or was psychological.

Her sense of guilt therefore seems like a personal illness. But, like Harry, once she is convinced that it is universal (original sin, again), she is free to move outside herself and to fight it in the world. She too goes out to become a missionary, and meets a terrible death. Her special quality is equated by Eliot with an ability to see below the ordinary surface of cocktail-party life. Her apparent illness is a 'vision'. She can take two courses. She can either forget her vision, 'be cured', return to 'normal' life; or she can follow her vision deeper and deeper along the path to sainthood. She takes the more painful course.

This is the same contrast as in *The Family Reunion*, with the ground splitting open beneath Pall Mall, but there is a difference. In the earlier play there was a sharp and rather unChristian distinction between those who understood and those who did not. The former were the only ones capable of self-fulfilment and the latter were dismissed out of hand. Harry's brother, John, was an inferior creature, useful only for running the estate. There was, in fact, a separate élite comparable to Anouilh's. In *The Cocktail Party* Celia is of this élite, like Harry; but the others are no longer dismissed. Eliot, it would seem, had come to accept self-fulfilment on a lower level. So the psychiatrist-confessor tells Lavinia Chamberlayne, who is nervous before her cocktail party:

> It is your appointed burden. And as for the party
> I am sure it will be a great success.

He even refuses to say which sort of self-fulfilment is better. 'Both ways are necessary.'

So Eliot's meaning keeps pace in this play with the further step which he has taken into the conventional drawing-room. It is impossible to say whether his views changed and the convention was ideally suited to express the change, or whether the convention has in some fiendish way overwhelmed him; in either case the process is fascinating to watch. But the extra degree of naturalism brought one special snag. Eliot likes to have adviser-confidants around his central characters. In *Murder in the Cathedral* they were formalized—the Priests and their opposites, the Tempters. In *The Family Reunion* Agatha was a deeply serious and faintly mysterious figure, still on the verge of the supernatural. But the Guardians in *The Cocktail Party* are strictly earth-bound, mixing drinks, cooking omelettes and cracking jokes; always in the very best of humour. Inevitably therefore, as they bustle round organizing their friends' salvation, there is a strong tinge of tea-party evangelism about their efforts. When they have successfully rehabilitated the Chamberlaynes they announce that they must now visit 'the Gunnings'. One's twinge of pity for the Gunnings reflects backwards over the whole play.

All Eliot's plays show individuals coming to a state of honesty and moving on towards self-fulfilment 'on the other side of despair'—he too, like Anouilh, used the phrase before

Sartre. For some of his characters this progress is a purely secular experience, for others it is raised by the Christian allusions into Expiation and Redemption. His last two plays are faint echoes of this theme, but here the élite, the potential saints, have quite vanished. The bourgeois characters and the domestic convention have pushed them, together with the poetry, right off the scene. In *The Confidential Clerk* (1953) young Colby makes the change from a business life to an artistic one—though only as a second-rate organist—when he discovers that his father too was an unsuccessful musician. The pattern is the same as Harry Monchensey's, but the scale minimal. Even the Christian allusions are still there, however faint. A character comments that Colby seems the sort of young man who will soon be reading for Orders.

The Elder Statesman (1958) is a better play than *The Confidential Clerk* because the symbols have now openly become those of the conventional post-Ibsen framework. Thus the change in the middle-aged characters since their youth is represented by their now using assumed names, the elder statesman's guilt appears in the form of two blackmailers whom he wronged long ago, and his present uneasy retirement, after a life devoted entirely to public success, is symbolized by his empty engagement book. The play therefore has a clear co-ordination of meaning and form, which *The Confidential Clerk* lacked, but it never seems deeply felt. Compared with the agony of *Ghosts*, which also concerns the disastrous results of trying to cloak immorality in respectability, *The Elder Statesman* seems like a sand-table reconstruction of a battle.

In *Poetry and Drama* (the Theodore Spencer Lecture at Harvard, 1950) Eliot emphasized the ability of poetic drama to capture the elusive in life, comparing it to the vision out of the corner of the eye. Poetically this is true—it is the way images work—but it becomes merely perverse in a naturalistic framework. In *The Family Reunion* Harry insists constantly on the uselessness of his trying to explain what he means—he wants to retain his elusiveness. This was the inevitable reaction of a poetic character to the assault of the prose characters around him, and of Eliot's poetry itself to the naturalistic convention

in which he was trying to set it. Harry *is* explicable in the terms
of the prose characters. His decision involves various actions—
becoming a missionary, doing specific things in specific places
—and these the others could grasp on their own level, even with
an inkling of his reasons. Yet Harry refuses to explain himself in
these terms because he knows that he will be emaciated in
the process: poetry refuses to pay the price of being paraphrased
in prose. By the time of *The Elder Statesman* this refusal has been
completely swept away. The resulting play is clear but thin.

Even so the echoes, both classical and Christian, persist.
Eliot's most recent line of dialogue, the last line of *The Elder
Statesman*, is spoken by the daughter of the elder statesman, a
man whose mundane Eumenides are two blackmailers. She
says to her fiancé:

> I feel utterly secure
> In you; I am a part of you. Now take me to my father.

Eliot the poet-dramatist is like a political prisoner who
obstinately continues to mouth, however faintly, his beliefs.
The irony is that Eliot's prison is of his own devising.

F *

16

Tennessee Williams 1914–

THE word most apt for Tennessee Williams' theatre is 'evocative'. He is a painterly dramatist who builds up a play with a
variety of delicate brush-strokes. These may be symbols, linked
images, sound effects off-stage, the sudden eruption of laughter,
the sigh of a snatch of music, the interruption of a scene by
some mysteriously poetic character, or even the play of electric
lights. He has compared himself to the painter in Shaw's *The
Doctor's Dilemma*, whose creed was 'the might of design, the
mystery of colour'. The meaning of a play, continues Williams,
resides 'in those abstract beauties of form and colour and line,
to which I would add light and motion'.[34] He is the modern
dramatist who most nearly shares Gordon Craig's ideal of
'beauty' in the theatre.

His first play, *The Glass Menagerie* (1945), is the most delicate of
his water-colours. The title gives its central symbol and its tone.
Laura is a girl of twenty-three whose lameness has confined her
in a brittle world of her own. She keeps with loving care a
collection of little glass animals, her menagerie, and she herself
is associated with the unicorn, different from the others because
of its horn. This glass menagerie can provide Williams with
many delicate touches. A young 'gentleman caller' is finally
enticed to the house by Laura's mother and brother, but he
deeply hurts this fragile girl by helping her some of the way off
the shelf and then dropping her. He makes her dance, he makes
her laugh, he even kisses her—all before revealing that he is
engaged. When he urges her to dance she protests that she is
too clumsy.

> Laura: Oh, but I'd step on you!
> Jim: I'm not made out of glass.
> Laura: How—how—how do we start?

Williams' touch there is perfect. He does not labour the image, and Jim's remark would seem quite natural in the context even if the symbol of the glass menagerie did not exist. At other times his use of it is heavier. During the dance they bump into the table and the unicorn's horn gets broken off. It has become a normal animal, just as Laura is becoming normal in this man's arms. But the pair of them discuss this event, this becoming 'less freakish' on the part of the unicorn, at some length—in effect, merely elucidating the analogy for the audience. The writing is good enough for the scene to succeed; but it is already an evident danger in Williams' method.

The Glass Menagerie does not, however, rely for its effect on its symbols. Its evocative clarity comes chiefly from the perfectly tuned language in which each of the four parts is written, from the nostalgic echoes of her youth in the mother's speeches, to the confident jargon of the gentleman caller's. Just as the whole play is refined away from reality without ever seeming unreal, so the characteristics of these four people are successfully heightened without ever toppling over into caricature.

A Streetcar Named Desire (1947) is somewhat tougher. In some ways the characters are similar to those of the earlier play but they are much more powerfully drawn. The central drama is the clash between Blanche Dubois and her brother-in-law, Stanley Kowalski. Blanche has Laura's fragility and, like Laura's mother, she clings pathetically to her faded shreds of Southern gentility. At the end of The Glass Menagerie Laura's brother Tom broke up the family because he was determined to travel round the world and to live life to the full. Stanley Kowalski would have left far sooner. He is a violent creature who indulges every extreme of anger or love. To delicate Blanche he seems a great ape. The clash between these two, with him enraged by her affectation and with her appalled by his roughness, is very dramatic and is excellently developed by Williams. Their antipathy has undertones of flirtation, initiated by her but leading eventually to rape; at the same time it has overtones of the struggle between social groups, the old and the new, the decadent and the virile, butterflies and apes. It makes, therefore, a very rich centre to the play.

A *Streetcar Named Desire* has often seemed ambiguous on the stage. Does Williams sympathize with Blanche or with Stanley? Without very careful direction this uncertainty can ruin the play, because in the early scenes an audience tends to share Stanley's fury with the affectations of Blanche and then suddenly finds its sympathies switching exclusively to Blanche because Stanley seems too outrageously cruel when he tells her fiancé, her last hope in life, that she has at one time been a prostitute. The film of the play certainly had this sudden break, but in reading the text one sympathizes more consistently with Stanley's growing rage. Williams' own remark about this play—'Watch out, or the apes will take over the world'—has often been used to make Stanley the villain of the piece, but it should not be taken too seriously. Blanche expresses the same attitude, even using the word 'ape' to describe Stanley, but she does so in a speech which is, in context, neurotically exaggerated. The truth is that the play is ambiguous in the best sense. Williams sympathizes with both of his characters, but his feeling for Blanche is one of pity, and for Stanley something nearer to fascinated admiration. It is the same conclusion as *The Glass Menagerie*, in which Laura's suffering is pitiable but Tom's determination to go out into the world and to live is right, even though it increases Laura's suffering. All the early plays of Tennessee Williams end by stressing the importance of living life to the full.

These first two plays remain his best. In each of them he had used off-stage effects to point the action. In *The Glass Menagerie* a thunderstorm punctuates the gentleman caller's visit: in *Streetcar* a honky-tonk piano mirrors each change of mood and, when Blanche's pretensions are finally shattered, a passing street-vendor is heard calling: '*Flores. Flores para los muertos*' . . . 'Flowers. Flowers for the dead.' These effects, though frequent, were used with sufficient tact. In *Summer and Smoke* (1948) they begin to loom too large: they dominate the drama, instead of reinforcing it. So, for example, the heroine first falls for the hero at a firework display and fireworks go up in the sky every time her feelings are made to soar by his remarks.

In texture *Summer and Smoke* is like *The Glass Menagerie*, but the delicate filigree of symbols has become more extensive. There is hardly a line or object or event which does not take its precise place in the pattern. Alma, a shy, soulful girl ('*alma*' is Spanish for 'soul') is afraid of physical love. She is symbolized by a stone angel in the middle of a fountain. John, the young doctor whom she loves, is frightened of spirituality and lives by indulging all his physical senses. His symbol is an anatomical chart on the wall of his study. With a heavy explicitness reminiscent of O'Neill, Williams has each symbol lit up at relevant moments in the development of the plot—in which Alma and John eventually convert each other. Alma comes to desire physical love, but John has meanwhile repented of his rake's progress and now accepts her as a special spiritual friend: he has become engaged to a more straightforwardly happy girl. So their see-sawing prevents their love from being fulfilled, but Alma, instead of committing suicide as she has planned, strikes up a temporary affair with a young travelling salesman. Life has won again.

The Rose Tattoo (1951) carries one stage further all these, by now, very recognizable characteristics, and adds a new element of grotesque farce. A goat is heard bleating whenever sexual activity is in the air: at two climactic moments of passion it even escapes and causes havoc. The rose of the title, which has also acquired a sexual connotation, crops up on almost every page, in the form of roses, a rose-shaped tattoo, the name Rosa, rose-water, rose-coloured glasses and a rose silk shirt. This shirt takes part in the final apotheosis of the symbol. When Serafina, a passionate widow who has been faithful to her husband Rosario's memory for three years, at last plans to take a lover again, the rose-coloured shirt is passed rapidly from hand to hand up a slope to the man. The stage-direction reads:

> The brilliantly coloured shirt moves in a zig-zag course through the pampas grass to the very top of the embankment, like a streak of flame shooting up a dry hill.

—in other words, the flame of sex shooting up the dry hill of three years' abstinence. Williams' approach to a play has become that of an imagist poet to his poem, and his approach to the audience has become almost Pavlovian—establish a symbol and present it whenever salivation is required. In *The Rose Tattoo* he is still ostensibly finding motivation for the symbols in his plot (the lover needs a shirt), but they are threatening to swamp the plot altogether. With *Camino Real* they do so.

Williams described the writing of *Camino Real* (1953) as being a 'release' for him. It releases, in fact, the full flood of symbols and theatrical effects which had been mounting up in his plays until it had to split their fairly conventional form at the seams. It is a sprawling and fanciful parable about middle age and the decay of dreams, of ideals, of youth. The title, characteristically, contains a pun which is also a symbol and is central to the play. In Spanish it means 'royal roadway', and the action takes place at the point where the roadway of life changes from royal to real. Characters like Casanova, Marguerite Daumier, Baron Charlus, Kilroy, Byron and Don Quixote all struggle with the difficulties of this special place. Most of them succumb to hopelessness, to a sort of fairy-tale *Iceman Cometh* existence; only one or two stride bravely on into the desert. The play has superb speeches and some excellent scenes—Williams is in many ways a transatlantic cousin of Anouilh's, not least in the sense that one can always rely on him for brightness of image and language—but as a whole *Camino Real* is a tantalizing hotch-potch. Excellent fantasy is frequently punctured by routine satire of modern life; and the meaning, in intention poetically mysterious, is too often merely obscure or else downright obvious.

Since *Camino Real* Williams has given up his extensive use o̟ symbols but he has never again achieved the certainty of form of his earlier work. The impact of *Cat on a Hot Tin Roof* (1955), commercially his most successful play since *Streetcar*, comes almost entirely from the violence of its characterization.

It is a hard play to describe, since it contains several separate themes, none of them fully dealt with or fully integrated with the others. Maggie the Cat is the sex-starved wife of Brick, a one-time college hero who has not slept with her since she revealed the latent homosexual love between him and his best friend and thus caused the latter's suicide. She tries to get Brick into her bed in the first scene of the play and succeeds in the last; but between these moments her problem is not in the foreground. Then there are the twin problems of Brick's alcoholism and his father's cancer. Both these unpleasant facts have to be faced, and in the second act each man forces the truth on the other. But again the theme is not followed up. Both suffer a violent shock of realization, but when we see Brick again it has made no difference to him and in one version of the play Big Daddy never even reappears. Finally the third act centres on Big Mama's being forced to face the truth about the cancer and on the two sons and their wives fighting over who shall inherit the estate. The play, in fact, is a series of violent 'moments' of the most dramatic type. The repercussions of each moment are lost in the drama of the next. Williams admits as much when he says in one of his stage-directions:

> The bird that I hope to catch in the net of this play is not the solution of one man's psychological problem. I'm trying to catch the true quality of experience in a group of people, that cloudy, flickering—fiercely charged!—interplay of live human beings in the thundercloud of a common crisis.

'Fiercely charged' sums up the play's merit and 'flickering' its limitation.

Since then none of Williams' plays has been worth very serious consideration. *Orpheus Descending* (1957) was a revised version of his first professionally produced play, *Battle of Angels*, which closed on tour in 1940 before reaching New York. It is in the style of the early plays but lacks their polish. Its many symbols are either crude or disjointed and the play gives the impression of being too closely linked to events in the author's own life and therefore of sharing the confusion of real life. Only its language and imagery, once again, redeem it—such as the image of the hero's freedom-loving spirit, a bird so light and with such huge wings that it even sleeps in the air and never touches the ground until it dies.

Suddenly Last Summer (1958) carried this brightness of imagery to excessive lengths. The play consists virtually of two short stories. Each is a woman's version of her life with a would-be poet, Sebastian, and each contains one violent central image. His mother pictures him as a detached aesthete. With her he saw a sight in the Encantadas which he took for an image of God and the world: great sea-birds were swooping down on newly hatched turtles as they scurried across the beach for the safety of the sea, and were turning them over on their backs to tear and devour their tender flesh. The beautiful Catherine's story of Sebastian goes deeper and presents him as much less detached. Instead of the observer he is now, in a sense, the turtle. He is a neurotic pederast (in inclination, if not in practice), terrified of the world and yet fiercely desiring it; and to attract the boys of his fancy he makes Catherine wear a bathing-suit which the water turns transparent. The central image of her story is his death in a blindingly hot white street, where he was killed and partially devoured by a gang of small boys. The mother's image was merely an observed experience, this one is suffered—fully so. The colours get brighter and fiercer in the girl's description until the mere recital of the event is a hysterical imagistic ecstasy.

These two stories are very loosely hung upon a vague plot about Sebastian's will, and are dramatized one after the other by the clumsy expedient of making a doctor murmur: 'Yes . . . and then?' and other such minor encouragements between each chunk of the ladies' narrative. Thus any exotic value which they might acquire in short-story form is effectively dispelled by the dramatization. *Sweet Bird of Youth* (1959) returns to the theme of *Camino Real*—the use, abuse and passing of youth. Melodramatic in form, it has at times a genuine savagery of disgust, at others something nearer to a gleeful indulgence in images of pain, futility and destruction.

It is a commonplace that Williams' plays have been growing more and more violent. In *A Streetcar Named Desire* it was the suicide of her young homosexual husband which first unsettled Blanche Dubois, and an almost identical experience is behind Maggie's troubles in *Cat on a Hot Tin Roof*. But these incidents are a valid part of the two women's stories, whereas the later plays seem purely sensational. *Suddenly Last Summer* contains every sort of physical and sexual shock. There are suggestions of incest and flagellation, open statements of pederasty and cannibalism. Even the set contains 'massive tree-flowers that suggest organs of a body, torn out, still glistening with undried blood' and the off-stage noises, which once came from honky-tonk pianos or street-vendors, are now the shrieks of jungle birds. The play takes place in a tropical jungle-garden which suits its atmosphere of festering heat. In *Sweet Bird of Youth*, apart from the excitements of mob violence (taken over from *Orpheus Descending*, in which a character was eaten by the lynchers' dogs), the hero and the heroine both, at separate times, have their sexual organs removed. To indicate how unmotivated all this is, it is sufficient to ask why, in *Suddenly Last Summer*, the sight of a woman in a transparent bathing-suit is likely to attract, at any rate exclusively, the sort of crowd which a pederast hopes for. As a practical move it has little to recommend it. But the idea is shockingly exciting, and that, it would seem, is enough.

Frederick Lumley, in *Trends in Twentieth-Century Drama*, uses Williams' own statement 'I prefer tenderness, but brutality seems to make better copy' to explain this development. But, again, the remark should not be taken too seriously. If his eye had been purely on the box-office, Williams could have made a much more commercial and, in this particular case, a much better play out of the material of *Suddenly Last Summer*. As it is, it seems even more of a frenzied personal statement than any of his other plays. The reason for the violence must go deeper. In his introduction to *Sweet Bird of Youth* Williams suggests that it results from his fear of the world, and that his violent plays are, therefore, in the nature of 'defiant aggressions' against the world. He claims that he derives a cathartic effect from his expression of violence. The audience, however, is unlikely to share this reaction; and it seems improbable that Williams will write another good play until he has worked this quality out of his system, or at least harnessed it, in the way that *Camino Real* worked out another, more stylistic, extreme. But *Sweet Bird of Youth*, so similar in theme to *Camino Real*, may have done this.

17

Arthur Miller 1915–

TENNESSEE WILLIAMS and Arthur Miller are almost invariably linked in people's minds and in books of criticism, for no better reason than that they are both American dramatists and both achieved world fame at about the same time. Beyond this they have almost nothing in common. Williams could more suitably be grouped with Lorca and Anouilh, while Miller develops an American tradition which he derives directly from Clifford Odets and Lillian Hellman. Williams is frequently judged, particularly in the United States, to be the greater of the two. He is seen as the true emotional artist, spinning webs of silk from his own suffering and environment, while Miller seems the mere intellectual craftsman who will take any challenging subject and make a play of it. Yet, paradoxically, Miller's plays strike deeper than the majority of Williams'. Williams' method militates against depth, because his symbols hold hands and dance neatly on the surface but set up few deeper reverberations. Miller, on the other hand, though his initial impulse may be intellectual and even didactic, is such a good dramatist that his carefully planned characters spring into life and far outrun their author's intentions. And even though his plays have widely different settings, one finds his own personal preoccupations at the centre of each of them, embedded often more deeply than Williams'.

His first successful play, *All My Sons* (1947), shows signs of the most careful, almost academic, planning. It is an Ibsen-like story of guilt from the past permeating and destroying the present. Joe Keller is an industrialist. His double crime is that during the war he sold the government a batch of faulty cylinder heads, which caused the death of twenty-one pilots, and later laid all the blame on his innocent manager, Deever. Deever is still in gaol, but Keller, although temporarily ruined, has again become a prosperous citizen. The characters are carefully graded to draw every last irony and implication from the story. Those whose careers suffered from their fighting in the war are balanced against others who prospered by staying behind. There are some who were once idealistic, some who still are, some who never were. And the emotional tangles of the situation are concentrated by the fact that the Keller and Deever families have always been close friends: young Chris Keller and Ann Deever are even in love. So the parallels and the contrasts provide frequent dramatic opportunities; Keller, for instance, is effectively horrified when he hears Ann Deever's violent denunciation of her father. But such detailed planning can well become arid. It is Miller's powerful characterization, strongly tinged with sympathy in every case, which saves it from being so.

Central to the play is the theme of betrayal. Keller has glossed over his betrayal of society with the old argument that everybody has to take risks in business, but his failing becomes unmistakable when it has repercussions on the personal level. His son Chris says:

> I know you're no worse than most men but I thought you were better. I never saw you as a man. I saw you as a father.

Keller has betrayed his responsibility as a parent and the climax of the play is the discovery that his elder son, thought to have been lost in action in the war, committed suicide at the news of his father's crime. There is betrayal in the other direction too, that of parents by their children. Miller evokes very powerfully the misery of the innocent Deever in gaol: in their idealistic disgust neither of his children has ever written to him or visited him. This betrayal of one's family responsibilities is a theme which Miller feels very deeply. He stresses it again in *Death of a Salesman*, in which Biff is shattered at discovering his father with a prostitute, and in which Willy Loman's suffering is greatly increased by his sons' lack of charity.

In *All My Sons*, as in all Miller's plays, society and the

individual are closely interrelated, not only in the effect of Keller's crime, which has such violent repercussions on both levels, but also in its cause. For, though the responsibility is entirely Keller's own, the pressures of a materialist society loomed large behind his decision. His reason for not telling the government that the cylinder heads were faulty (though, he thought, harmlessly so) was that he would lose his large contract, and a lifetime accumulation of business know-how might be wasted. Similarly, Keller was made most aware of his guilt by neighbours shouting 'Murderer!' at him in the street, and he glories in his renewed success when the very same people start playing poker with him again. The respect which Miller's heroes long for is not so much their own as society's. Give me my 'name', they all insist. The individuality they crave must be endorsed by their neighbours.

This is particularly true of Willy Loman, the hero of *Death of a Salesman* (1949). The whole life of the Loman family is dominated by this man's idea of 'success', which he sees as a ladder leading from a brilliant athletic career at school to a good job and a life surrounded by scores of influential friends and admiring neighbours. He is mesmerized by two romantic images of this success: one of his brother Ben, who walked into the jungle at seventeen and walked out again, rich, at twenty-one; and the other of an eighty-four-year-old salesman who was still so popular that in any of thirty cities he could just pick up the phone and wait comfortably in his hotel room for the buyers to come to him. Loman wants only the very best for his two sons, who are the centre of his life, but, driven by these images of success, he spoils them, overlooks their dishonesty and tortures them with his ambition for them. They come to despise him, until Biff, the elder of the two, at last throws over the whole pretence of his having an exceptional future and asserts his independence, his right to fail. In the explosion Willy Loman suddenly sees how deeply his son could care for him. This discovery pushes him to the final extreme of his illusion. Crying out: 'That boy—that boy is going to be magnificent!' and: 'Ben, he'll worship me for it!' he drives out to commit suicide so that Biff shall collect the twenty thousand dollars from his life insurance and be able to go into business. 'When the mail comes he'll be ahead of Bernard again,' he says. Bernard is the neighbour's successful son. Once again the pressures of society have distorted and destroyed the human relationships.

Death of a Salesman is an admirable blend of pathos and satire. There has been much argument about whether or not it is a tragedy. It is not; but the reasons offered, and Miller's answers to them, have been mainly spurious. The play is non-tragic, not because it has a modern setting with talk of refrigerators and insurance policies, nor even, necessarily, because the hero dies in the full flush of his illusion, but simply because Willy Loman lacks the ferocity which is an essential ingredient of tragedy, and because his driving illusion is one which we do not respect. The mainsprings of the great tragedies—lust, ambition, jealousy— are forces which we fully respect, but Willy Loman's neurotic awareness of the difference between being 'liked' and being 'well liked', and his identification of success with a cheering crowd round a football field, are attitudes which, even though we ourselves may live by them, we at least profess to scorn. Without Arthur Miller's deep sympathy a creature held in thrall by them would be the pure stuff of satire, the one character omitted by Ben Jonson from *The Alchemist*. Willy Loman is more than that because he evokes pity. But he cannot evoke terror.

Miller has been particularly ill-used by critics. Even Eric Bentley, normally a reliable pundit, has written of *Death of a Salesman*:

> One never knows what a Miller play is about; politics or sex. If *Death of a Salesman* is political, the key scene is the one with the tape-recorder; if it is sexual, the key scene is the one in the Boston hotel.[35]

Bentley is presenting as a defect one of the play's main merits— that it is about both politics *and* sex, that both scenes (and several others) are key scenes, that the individual drama and the social are inextricably fused. Continuing, he does precisely the same thing for *The Crucible* (1953):

You may say of *The Crucible* that it isn't about McCarthy, it's about love in the seventeenth century.

Again he points out the play's excellence and calls it a flaw, complying with the general American reaction to *The Crucible*, which, it was somehow thought, had to be actually *about* McCarthy. Joseph Wood Krutch expresses this attitude when he writes:

> *The Crucible* laid its scene at the time of the Salem witch trials with the obvious intention of drawing a parallel between them and the 'security trials' of the present day. Its validity depends upon the validity of the parallel and those who find it invalid point out that, whereas witchcraft was pure delusion, subversion is a reality, no matter how unwisely or intemperately it may be combatted.[36]

This is, of course, ridiculous. *The Crucible*'s validity in no sense depends on the validity of the parallel, though it is understandable that the date of its appearance, 1953, should have made its first critics judge it by the narrow standards of topicality. Its only connection with the security trials is that Miller's own experience of the McCarthy scare (and he has described how his friends were soon cutting him in the streets[37]) was the stimulus for a play about mass hysteria and the individual caught up in its evil.

This individual is John Proctor, a Salem farmer. The witch-hunt begins when a group of girls are found dancing naked in the woods. They discover that the best way of avoiding punishment is to pretend that they are possessed; but to prove their possession they need to name people whom they have seen in the company of the devil. They name a few. So the snowball starts. John Proctor becomes involved in two ways; first as a responsible citizen concerned with opposing this evil, secondly, and more important, because he once committed adultery with Abigail, the oldest of the possessed girls, when she was a maid in his house. His wife discovered this and turned her out. Abigail still loves Proctor, but he has repented and will have nothing to do with her. Not surprisingly, once Abigail discovers the power of being possessed, Elizabeth Proctor is soon named as a witch. Proctor defies the court in her defence and is himself named by the girls as 'the Devil's man'.

In gaol his deepest dilemma appears. He is condemned with two others, Rebecca Nurse and Martha Corey, and their fate is crucial to the whole situation in Salem. The condemned are executed only if they refuse to confess that they have had traffic with the devil. In these circumstances many of the victims have confessed, but these three are the first whose integrity would, in normal times, have been beyond doubt. If they confess, the whole witch-hunt will be given the stamp of authenticity. Clearly they must die in silence. Proctor's dilemma is that he is haunted by the guilt of his adultery and feels he would be a fraud if he shared the martyrdom of the others. A meeting with his pregnant wife, in which she admits that her own coldness prompted his adultery, decides him to make a false confession to this false court. He retracts it, however, when he hears that it will be nailed to the door of the church just before the others die.

> I blacken all of them when this is nailed to the church the very day they hang for silence,

he says, adding, like all Miller's heroes,

> How may I live without my name?

He cannot even perjure himself alone. His actions inevitably involve the rest of his community, and he dies with the others. Miller adds, in a postscript, that very soon 'the power of theocracy in Massachusetts was broken'.

The Crucible rises to its heights on the personal level, in Proctor's tragic predicament, but once again the social and the personal are tightly interwoven. This was made particularly clear by Sartre's film version of the play, *The Witches of Salem* (1956), in which he tipped the main emphasis on to the social without in any way distorting the implications of the original. Miller had used Ibsen's method of piecemeal revelation, gradually filling in details from the past throughout the play. Sartre took these details, arranged them in chronological order, and was left with a narrative which moved perfectly from the individual to the whole society and, at the very end, back to the individual. It started with Elizabeth Proctor's puritanical dogmatism and lack of love pushing Proctor into his adultery. From this one home the story expanded to involve the whole community of which Elizabeth's faults were symptomatic, then followed the gruesome course of the persecution which those faults made possible, and finally showed the return to sanity prompted by the stand of John Proctor and the others. With the crowd storming the prison and cutting down their bodies the evil began to be purged from the society, just as it had now been purged in Elizabeth herself. At the end of the film she prevents an angry group of men from attacking Abigail and thus pointlessly prolonging the evil. At least she loved him, she argues.

A Memory of Two Mondays (1955) is Miller's simplest play and would appear to be his most purely autobiographical. The others seem autobiographical in the sense that the themes which haunt him are buried deep in each new subject, but this one-act play expresses directly the experience of an intelligent young man doing manual labour amongst a group of people who are condemned for ever to a hard way of life which he himself will rise out of. It is admirably written. It suggests superbly the dreariness of these routine lives, together with the great kindness and mutual loyalty which make them tolerable. It deftly sketches in unhackneyed characters and manages to draw the wider implications without seeming pretentious. Finally, it is never sentimental. At the end, when the young man is setting off to a better job, the others obstinately refuse to fulfil his hopes of an emotional farewell scene.

In the Broadway production A View from the Bridge (1955) made up the double bill with A Memory of Two Mondays. Since then Miller has turned it into a full-length play. It is comparable to Death of a Salesman, but it has the ferocity which the earlier play lacked and so can more nearly be described as tragic (The Crucible is a full-scale tragedy by any criterion.) It is the story of a New York longshoreman, Eddie Carbone, and of his jealous love for his niece and ward, Catherine. He is sheltering two Italian immigrants, relations of his wife, who have entered the country illegally. Rodolpho, the younger of them, and Catherine fall in love. Eddie fights their engagement with everything he can think of. He tries to prove that Rodolpho is a homosexual, and he argues that he wants an American wife only for the sake of an American passport. He refuses to admit the real reason for his opposition—that he himself loves the girl. Finally he tips off the police about the immigrants. When Marco, the older one, is arrested, he spits in Eddie's face and accuses him of betraying them. Eddie calls him a liar, demands an apology, fights him and is killed.

The power of the play is in the wild power of Eddie himself. He is a man possessed, a man who refuses to 'settle for half', and he reveals yet another recurrent theme of Miller's—that of the tragic force of obsession. In his Preface to his *Collected Plays* Miller used precisely the same phrase of Willy Loman, that of refusing to 'settle for half', and also said that if he rewrote *The Crucible* he would make the judge's obsession with his holy and wholly evil task much more central.

But *A View from the Bridge* contains all the familiar themes too—of loyalty, of betrayal, and of the need for a name, for public esteem. Answering Marco's shouted challenge: 'Eddie Carbone!' Eddie yells his own name straight back:

> Yeah. Marco! Eddie Carbone. Eddie Carbone. Eddie Carbone.

and continues

> Wipin' the neighbourhood with my name like a dirty rag! I want my name, Marco.

Marco, when he lunges at him with the knife, thrusts with it the one word 'Animal!' It sums up Eddie Carbone. His magnificence is an animal magnificence. So is the play's.

Miller, however, makes the mistake of rationalizing this in

the mouth of the lawyer, Alfieri, who acts as a commentator and who speaks the play's last words:

> Most of the time now we settle for half and I like it better. But the truth is holy, and even as I know how wrong he was, and his death useless, I tremble, for I confess that something perversely pure calls to me from his memory— not purely good, but himself purely, for he allowed himself to be wholly known and for that I think I will love him more than all my sensible clients. And yet, it is better to settle for half, it must be! And so I mourn him—I admit it—with a certain . . . alarm.

These words give a very different impression from the play which they end. To say 'the truth is holy' and 'he allowed himself to be wholly known' about a man who betrayed his relations for a reason which he refused to face, and then called anyone who accused him of having done so a liar, is, to say the least, misleading. 'Himself purely' is nearer the mark, but it is not the predominant impression given by the speech. This *explication de texte* confuses the play, seeming irrelevant in the same way as some of Miller's comments on Willy Loman in his Preface seem irrelevant to *Death of a Salesman*. But they, being outside it, are unable to spoil the play.

Miller's output has been small (four full-length plays and one one-act) but it has maintained a very high standard. He is a dramatist of passion, conviction and intelligence. His prose, though less highly coloured than Williams', has a muscularity which enables it to be put to the most weighty purposes without seeming bombastic. Williams' dialogue often provides a better definition of character, but Miller's has a different sort of 'right-ness'—that of being exactly appropriate to its dramatic context. His language changes more from play to play and from scene to scene than from character to character. Above all he has the same genius as T. S. Eliot (in his poetry) for the simple, even drab, statement at the moment of climax. So Willy Loman pronounces, 'That boy—that boy is going to be magnificent!' and Elizabeth Proctor says, in her great confession to Proctor,

'It needs a cold wife to prompt lechery . . . It were a cold house I kept.' Unfortunately Miller is a dramatist who needs an outside stimulus to provide the framework for his own pre-occupations—the McCarthy episode produced *The Crucible* and a chance newspaper story *A View from the Bridge*—and these stimuli seem few and far between.

18

The New Playwrights

THIS final chapter deals individually with the more interesting playwrights to have appeared in the last ten years. Some of them occupy a disproportionate amount of space in a book where Elmer Rice, Clifford Odets, O'Casey, Salacrou and Betti have not been given individual attention. But these new authors are still writing. The critic is assessing their potential as much as their achievement. This, together with the topicality of his subject-matter, alters the tone of his criticism. Analysis of the plays becomes more lenient, more ephemeral—but not, for that reason at any rate, less interesting.

France

France is in the odd position of having a new generation, but no young generation, of playwrights. In a recent 'guide to contemporary French theatre' (Wallace Fowlie's *Dionysus in Paris*, 1961) the youngest author to be dealt with is Camus, who was born in 1912. The section on the new wave, entitled 'Experimental Theatre', contains comment on Artaud (born 1905), Beckett (1906), Adamov (1908), Genet (1909), Schéhadé (1910) and Ionesco (1912). This strange fact makes little difference to the exuberance of French theatre today. But it threatens an alarming hiatus fifteen years ahead.

The only three of these new French dramatists to have made an international mark are Samuel Beckett, Eugène Ionesco and Jean Genet. Beckett's *Waiting for Godot* is the most commercially successful 'experimental' play since *Six Characters in Search of an Author*. First produced in Paris in 1952, it has since been translated into eighteen languages and performed all over the world.

Its immediate appeal is due to the fact that, even though nothing much happens, it is intensely theatrical. The endless

cross-talk act of the two tramps is always funny and at the same
time sad—funny because good cross-talk acts are very funny,
and sad because their main reason for talking at all is just to
pass away the time, to fill in the void. Under the farcical ripple
of the dialogue lies a serious concern.

Vladimir: Where was I . . . How's your foot?

Estragon: Swelling visibly.

Vladimir: Ah, yes, the two thieves. Do you remember the
the story?

Estragon: No.

Vladimir: Shall I tell it to you?

Estragon: No.

Vladimir: It'll pass the time. (*pause*) It was two thieves,
crucified at the same time as our Saviour. One——

Estragon: Our what?

Vladimir: Our Saviour. Two thieves. One is supposed to
have been saved and the other . . . (*he searches for the contrary
of saved*) . . . damned.

Estragon: Saved from what?

Vladimir: Hell.

Estragon: I'm going. (*he does not move*)

Vladimir: And yet . . . (*pause*) . . . how is it—this is not boring
you I hope—how is it that of the four evangelists only
one speaks of a thief being saved? The four of them were
there—or thereabouts—and only one speaks of a thief
being saved. (*pause*) Come on, Gogo, return the ball,
can't you, once in a way?

Estragon: (*with exaggerated enthusiasm*). I find this really most
extraordinarily interesting.

Vladimir: One out of four. Of the other three, two don't
mention any thieves at all and the third says that both
of them abused him.

Estragon: Who?

Vladimir: What?

Estragon: What's all this about? (*pause*) abused who?

Vladimir: The Saviour.

Estragon: Why?

G

Vladimir: Because he wouldn't save them.
Estragon: From hell?
Vladimir: Imbecile! From death.
Estragon: I thought you said from hell.
Vladimir: From death, from death.
Estragon: Well, what about it?
Vladimir: Then the two of them must have been damned.
Estragon: And why not?
Vladimir: But the other Apostle says that one was saved.
Estragon: Well? They don't agree, and that's all there is to it.
Vladimir: But all four were there. And only one speaks of a thief being saved. Why believe him rather than the others?
Estragon: Who believes him?
Vladimir: Everybody. It's the only version they know.
Estragon: People are bloody ignorant apes.

This passage shows clearly Beckett's technique. Serious subject-matter is being presented in music-hall form. The genuine concern of one tramp with the possibility of salvation is constantly broken into by the other with remarks like 'I find this most extraordinarily interesting', and the discussion follows a carefully constructed comic pattern, with Vladimir's logic steadily tightening only to be punctured by Estragon's final 'People are bloody ignorant apes'. This tug between subject-matter and form runs through the whole play. Much of the surface is taken up with farcical satire of conventional social behaviour. Pozzo, for example, is unable to take a simple action like sitting down without an attendant barrage of ceremony; and the two tramps are always trying to strike up what will pass for a polite conversation, using catch-phrases like Vladimir's 'This is not boring you I hope?' But the satire is not mere incidental comedy. As with Eliot, the emphasis on the surface aspects of life has its part in the meaning of the play. At one point fat Pozzo is lying on the ground, unable to get up. Spasmodically he shouts 'Help!'. Vladimir, glad of this chance to be useful for once, says 'Let us not waste our time in idle discourse' and launches into a long speech. This is a typical Beckett scene. The situation itself is farcical and yet has serious implications; and Vladimir's speech, though mock-pompous in tone, contains the real meaning of the play. He says:

> What are we doing here, that is the question. And we are blessed in this, that we happen to know the answer. Yes, in this immense confusion one thing alone is clear. We are waiting for Godot to come—

and later:

> What's certain is that the hours are long, under these conditions, and constrain us to beguile them with proceedings which, how shall I say, which may at first sight seem reasonable until they become a habit. You may say it is to prevent our reason from foundering.

As with Eliot the surface 'proceedings' of life, of which the play is made up, keep mankind's attention off the despair beneath it all. But for Beckett this is a relief (however ironical), because he does not share Eliot's optimistic Christian faith in a redemption beyond the despair.

Waiting for Godot can be, and has been, given many different interpretations. However, having no one meaning is not at all synonymous with having no meaning. Beckett is a very eclectic writer. His play is full of obvious Christian echoes, but it also contains less marked historical and anthropological allusions. Each member of the audience picks up the echoes to which he is most attuned. My own interpretation is that the two tramps are two parts of a person or of a community seen subjectively, with Vladimir representing the more spiritual part and Estragon the more animal; and that Pozzo and Lucky make up a person or a community viewed objectively, Pozzo being the exploiter and the user of ideas, Lucky the exploited and the creator of ideas. In other words we suffer with Estragon and Vladimir, their fears, their hopes, their hatreds and loves; but we view Pozzo and Lucky through their eyes and therefore see in them only the social surface of life. But the question of which precise meaning Beckett had in mind is unimportant. What is important—and this is a factor which is common to nearly all the interpretations—is that these four characters should add up to a picture of humanity at large. This is essential because the play is, above all, about mankind's attempts to fiddle its way through life, setting up a wall of hopes and pretences between itself and despair. The greatest of these hopes—that there is some point to existence, that we are keeping some mysterious appointment on earth and are therefore not random scraps of life—is symbolized by Godot. Critics have asked many questions about the precise nature of Godot, but they are irrelevant questions. The play is not about Godot, but, as its title states, about the waiting for him. It is about life on earth, not hereafter.

Vladimir and Estragon successfully establish themselves as a true lowest common denominator of humanity. Their warmth in the middle of despair is the world's. This, together with its theatricality and the brilliance of its rhythms and language, makes *Waiting for Godot* a great play which will last. Beckett has not since reached such heights. *Endgame* (1957) is well written but the despair has become so all-pervading that the characters are no longer recognizable symbols of humanity. Beckett's other plays have all been extremely short. The best of them is *Krapp's Last Tape* (1959), in which an old man listens to a description of his one happy sexual experience, a description which he recorded on tape years ago in a series of beautifully delicate images, reminiscent of Molly Bloom.

Eugène Ionesco came to the theatre by way of platitude. He was inspired to write his first play by a book of English phrases, and the characters of *The Bald Prima Donna* (1950)—Mr and Mrs Smith, their maid Mary and their friends the Martins—were the characters in the elementary lessons. The play is a glorious symposium of the clichés of bourgeois social life, full of routine *non sequiturs*, polite amazement at banal facts, long rambling stories and an apparent eagerness to communicate, without any success. The only interesting subject in these people's lives is the mysterious bald prima donna, but when a visiting fireman asks how she is they are deeply shocked and immediately change the subject. The play, though it has weaknesses, is very funny.

Its value is that its fantasy is firmly rooted in banal but universal experience.

Ionesco's best plays all share this generality (it is the quality needed to add depth to his two-dimensional characters) but his second piece, *The Lesson* (1950), is not one of them. The story is of a professor trying to teach mathematics and comparative linguistics to a girl pupil. His mounting exasperation is paralleled by a pattern of mounting sexual interest, and the play ends with his symbolic rape and murder of the girl. But this teacher-pupil relationship fails to develop wider implications, and much of the time is taken up with logic-chopping, some of it genuinely comic, some merely clever, some futile. It is unfortunate that this play has become internationally popular, since it helps to foster the false idea that Ionesco's chief qualities are verbal anarchy, surprise for its own sake, and nonsense philosophizing. Ionesco himself has claimed that he has shattered language and is building it anew. But the jumbles of non-words into which his plays at times sink are more often mere vehicles for feeble and extraneous jokes.

The Lesson was followed by *The Chairs* (1952), a successfully theatrical study of an old married couple and their memories. Ionesco's plays were now becoming increasingly subjective, increasingly neurotic, increasingly general. *Jack or Submission* (1955) and its sequel, *The Future is in Eggs* (1957), are nightmare pictures of a young man suffering the various pressures brought to bear on him by his family—the pressure to conform, to keep up the family tradition and to breed an heir. The grisly comic effects derive from the way the characters perform their familiar routines even though the situations are farcical. So Jack is disowned until he is prepared to toe the family line and say he likes potatoes in their jackets; the obsession with the need for children is represented by his relations' putting dozens of eggs under him and rhythmically urging him on to hatch them. In *Victims of Duty* (1953) the little-man hero is forced by his wife and a policeman to delve painfully back into his memories. From facing his past honestly he derives a new freedom, which becomes evident in an alarming tendency to levitate out of reach of his wife and the policeman. He clearly needs more weight. The play ends with their forcibly feeding him on crusts of bread.

Amédée (1954) and *The New Tenant* (1956) are Ionesco's best plays. In them he fully externalizes his central characters' neuroses by attaching them to concrete symbols (the corpse in *Amédée*, the furniture in *The New Tenant*—see pages 78–9). These symbols have two excellent results. They keep the meaning general by demanding no specific interpretation; and they give the action a focal point, something often lacking in the earlier pieces. The objects are treated completely naturalistically (to *Amédée* and his wife the huge corpse is just that—a huge corpse) and this naturalism leaves no room for extraneous jokes. The verbal anarchy of the earlier plays disappears in these two.

After *The Killer* (*Tueur sans Gages*, 1958), a very disjointed affair, Ionesco produced his most commercially successful play—*Rhinoceros* (1959). The hero, Bérenger, is caught up in a world in which everyone is changing into a rhinoceros. By the end he is the only human being left. This allegory of herd hysteria (with occasional specific allusions to the rise of the Nazis) provides Ionesco with some excellent opportunities, especially in the characters' rationalization of the terrible events; Bérenger and a friend can seriously argue the pros and cons of changing into a rhinoceros, and the neighbours avoid taking alarm or action by indulging in a philosophical disputation on the precise number of animals which the available evidence can prove to be loose in the town. Here the logic-chopping is dramatically justified and very effective, but, even so, the play flags. The central symbol is less fertile than the corpse in *Amédée*.

In one scene of *Rhinoceros* Ionesco makes the serious mistake of showing a character physically changing before our eyes, with a horn growing from his head and his chest turning green. This bathos is typical of Ionesco, and similar errors of dramatic judgement occur in all his plays. Even *Amédée* collapses at the end, when Ionesco suddenly introduces several new characters and has Amédée flying up in the air, protesting weakly that he is 'against transcendence'. This is an amusing version of the classical exaltation at the end of a tragedy, but it should have been possible to end the play within its own compact set of symbols. In other plays irrelevant jokes are allowed to spoil scenes, good ideas are laboured and killed. Ionesco remains an amateur (in the English sense of the word) of the theatre.

Jean Genet's is a theatre of charade. He uses the ritual of dressing-up to express the duality of certain strong feelings—the love in the hatred, the envy in the scorn. The clearest example of this is his first performed play, *The Maids* (1947), in which two sisters, Claire and Solange, dress up in the clothes of their mistress, Madame, whenever she is out. They have evolved a ritual in which one of them, in her own rôle as a maid, helps the other to dress as Madame. She grovels to dust her shoe while Madame revels in her growing magnificence; then suddenly she spits on Madame and beats her to the ground. This orgy of sadism and masochism, of arrogance and humility, reflects perfectly the two maids' attitude to Madame, whom they are planning to kill. When she arrives she is not the ogre we have been expecting, but a fairly ordinary, rich, over-romantic, superficial woman of the world. Without drinking the poisoned tea which they offer her, she hurries out to pursue her ridiculously romanticized lover. The maids return to their ceremony. Claire now realizes that their first move against Madame must be to kill in themselves the elements of Madame which they so hate—her hypocritical superiority and her self-importance. Dressed as Madame she forces Solange to hand her the poisoned tea, and drinks it. Solange's final speech is, for the first time, honest and calm.

This makes an admirable and highly compact one-act play. It also exemplifies the dedicated amorality of Genet's work. Genet was an orphan, was sent very young to a remand home, and has had ten convictions for theft. Treated as an outcast, he became convinced that only hypocrisy made bourgeois society any different from himself. The evil which he felt in himself was the reality of the world, so to him every banker was a respectable thief, every nun a sublimated whore. His thefts were, in part, a flamboyant protest against this hypocritical morality, but in his late thirties he discovered a less inconvenient form of protest—literature. *The Maids* expresses perfectly Genet's idea of morality, in which self-fulfilment involves accepting and fostering one's intrinsically amoral nature. Solange's honesty at the end of the play is the honesty of vice—for the first time she admits openly and unashamedly her incestuous Lesbianism with her sister. Yet, oddly enough, this determinedly amoral play strikes an audience as being strongly moral. The stripping away of pretence is the familiar and necessary prelude to regeneration. One need not stop at the bottom with Genet.

The Blacks (1958) follows a similar pattern, the subject being the ambivalent attitude of negroes to whites. The negroes enact an elaborate ceremony, in which their desire to kill a white woman merges with their desire to impress her sexually. After the ritual murder of a white Queen, Judge, Governor and Missionary (played by negroes wearing white masks) the negroes at last become, like Claire and Solange, purely themselves. For the first time the central couple make love without secret overtones and without imitation. The girl says: 'At least we know that you can't twist your fingers in my long blonde hair.'

Genet's earlier full-length play, *The Balcony* (1956), is an analysis, equating power with sex, of similar figureheads of authority—Queen, Judge, Bishop, General and, the newcomer to the ranks, the Chief of Police. It is a far more searing assault on the Establishment than any left-wing English playwright has produced. The early scenes in the brothel, in which ordinary men are dressed up by prostitutes in the enormous robes of dignitaries and then enact with the girls their sexual fantasies of power, are the best charades which Genet has written. Later the analysis becomes too metaphysical and swamps the play. Genet's theatrical method is very limited, though within its own bounds it can be highly effective.

U.S.A.

In 1950 American theatre seemed to be leading the world. The twenties and thirties had been times of intense theatrical activity in the States, and now the forties had produced Tennessee Williams and Arthur Miller. Out of quantity, it seemed, there was emerging quality—an ideal situation.

A decade later the picture was very different. Williams' first two plays had turned out to be his best, Miller had lapsed into a six-year silence; and nobody, nobody at all, had stepped forward to follow them. William Inge, a low-brow Ibsen, writes commercial plays whose apparent seriousness presumably adds to their appeal. William Saroyan, a self-appointed Messiah who as long ago as 1939 heralded his first one-act play (*The Man with the Heart in the Highlands*) with the announcement 'The greater and truer American theatre shall begin its life after the appearance and influence of this play', has steadily bogged down in his own sentimentality. Two novelists, Truman Capote and Carson McCullers, made a brief excursion into the theatre with *The Grass Harp* and *The Member of the Wedding* and then bowed out again. Arthur Laurents wrote a few moderately successful plays before moving over to musical comedy and writing the book for *West Side Story* (1957) and *Gipsy* (1959).

More recently there has been William Gibson, another novelist, who turned to the theatre in his forties. His first play, *Two for the Seesaw* (1958), was a character comedy and a *tour de force* in that the cast numbered only two. A year later he dramatized a book of his own about Helen Keller's early life. *The Miracle Worker* (1959) shows Annie Sullivan's attempts to reach the mind of the deaf, dumb, blind and unruly child of seven. Theatrically it is very effective, and is saved from sentimentality by its factual subject-matter; but it is a product more of craft than of art. Gibson will become America's Terence Rattigan—a brilliant craftsman who can move from subject to subject, touching each with the magic wand of 'theatre' but developing no vision of his own.

The most recent American playwright is Jack Gelber, whose first play, *The Connection* (1960), greatly impressed New York but not London. It is about drug-addicts being pestered by interested and sympathetic outsiders. The play is spoilt by a pseudo-Pirandellian framework which has no consistency and which leads the author into several stylistic *impasses*, but the central naturalistic core, made up of the drifting dialogue of the 'junkies', is excellent, and indicates where Gelber's real vein may lie.

Switzerland

Since the Nazi régime no new playwright has emerged from Germany to win an international reputation, but German-speaking Switzerland has recently, and for the first time in its history, produced two important playwrights. The early plays of Friedrich Dürrenmatt (b. 1921) and Max Frisch (b. 1911) have little in common, but their recent and most successful works have affinities which are worth discussing. Dürrenmatt's *The Visit* (*Der Besuch der Alten Dame*, 1956) and Frisch's *The Fire Raisers* (1958) are modern bourgeois Moralities in reaction against the great German post-war prosperity, but they share none of the hysteria which the equivalent materialism of the twenties caused in the theatre.

In *The Visit* Claire Zachanassian, the richest old lady in the world, comes back to the small town of her birth. Everyone is hoping for a large gift for the city and its citizens, and at the banquet in her honour she duly offers them an impressive sum —but on one condition: they must kill Alfred Ill, an honoured citizen and the most likely choice for the next mayor. Her reason is that many years ago he disowned the baby she had by him, paid two men to swear, falsely, that they also had slept with her and so had her driven out of the town as a prostitute. Thus she started on the life of a courtesan which led, through several judicious marriages, to her millions; and now she is prepared to buy her revenge. The town's initial reaction to her proposal is one of high moral indignation, but the first act ends with her ominously calm words: 'I can wait.' Soon everyone is buying rich food and expensive clothes on credit. Since Ill himself is a shopkeeper he sees at first hand what is going on, but he can do nothing. Eventually, as the town's debts rise, pure economics make his death inevitable.

The play has weaknesses: there are too many repetitions of Ill discovering people wearing smart new clothes or shoes; and Dürrenmatt makes the citizens exaggeratedly callous. But its value lies in the vivid moral astringency, which comes from the central idea and from Dürrenmatt's free treatment of it in the generalized setting of a small town. The play can thus be both fantastic (Claire's arrival with her horrifying retinue of two blind eunuchs—the perjurers whom she has since used her wealth to capture, mutilate and retain—has an archetypal quality of doom) and at the same time modern (she receives a wedding telegram from President Eisenhower). The astringency is reflected in the language. Claire and her husband, on their hotel balcony, hear the row when Ill discovers what people are doing and throws all his customers out of his shop.

Husband VIII: Noise in the street.
Claire: Small-town life.
Husband VIII: Seems to be something wrong in the store down there.
Claire: Probably fighting over the price of meat.

In *The Fire Raisers* Max Frisch treats the subject of appeasement with similar astringency. Even the hero's name is itself in the tradition of medieval Moralities—it means Honest Man, and his Christian name is Gottlieb, Love of God. He is a good bourgeois living in a town in which there has recently been an inordinate amount of arson. He believes that all arsonists should be strung up; and an unemployed circus wrestler, called Schmitz, who calls at his door, somehow knows that these are his views. Schmitz begs a meal from the reluctant Biedermann, and finally is even allowed to sleep in the attic. The next day his equally disreputable friend moves into the attic too, and Biedermann and his wife, Babette, are kept awake by a trundling noise—petrol drums being rolled into place, it transpires. Biedermann makes two feeble attempts to get rid of the pair, but as it becomes more and more obvious that they are the arsonists, he grows, in his terror, increasingly charming towards them. Finally, determined to keep them friendly, he throws a goose dinner in their honour. At it they accuse him of suspecting them, and when he denies it they suggest that he prove his faith by lending them some matches (they have in fact forgotten theirs and are temporarily helpless). He does so. They burn the house down, and Biedermann and Babette find themselves, for the second half of the play, in Hell.

In high indignation Biedermann protests his bourgeois virtue.

> All my life I've kept the ten commandments. I've never made myself a brazen image, certainly not. I've never coveted my neighbour's house, or if I did covet it I bought it.

Finally he and Babette do get to Heaven, because, as the devil announces in disgust, there seems to have been a general amnesty. It has been decided that

> whoever wears a uniform or did wear a uniform when he killed, or whoever promises to wear a uniform when he kills or orders others to kill, is saved.

The play is specifically related to the rise of Nazism, the wartime destruction of Germany and the new prosperity. Biedermann says that the great fire has after all proved a blessing, 'city-planning-wise', and the Chorus conclude with:

> Finer than ever,
> Richer than ever,
> High modern towers
> Gleaming with glass and with chrome,
> Though at heart it is just as before,
> Hallelujah,
> Risen again is our city.

The poetry of Frisch's Chorus is often Brechtian in style. Frisch was a close friend of Brecht's, and *The Fire Raisers*, though at no point imitative, is the best development of Brecht's theatre to have yet appeared. It is a line of influence which should lead far.

Great Britain

May 8, 1956 is the most widely quoted date in recent British theatre criticism. It is the day on which the Royal Court Theatre presented John Osborne's *Look Back in Anger*. Since then a new life and excitement has entered the London theatre, which had been in a state of fitful hibernation since Shaw and Galsworthy. In the fifties it had reached an extreme of literary playfulness in the dramatic poetry of Christopher Fry, of which Osborne's prose was the violent opposite. Brash, impetuous, full of hyperboles and lashing out at every possible target, this prose had an animal vitality which was new at the time and has not since been equalled.

Vitality, in his characters as well as in their dialogue, is the great merit of Osborne's work. The weakness of his first plays lies in the more intellectual side of playwriting, in the organization of the whole play and in its meaning. The end of *Look Back in Anger*, for example, is particularly unsatisfactory. The real reason for Jimmy Porter's cruelty to his wife throughout the play has been his own excess of energy. His job in a sweet-stall uses hardly any of it and he vents the rest in abuse of Alison. He longs for a 'come-back', but she is too weak and gentle to provide it; she suffers in silence and his rage increases. Her friend Helena, who becomes Jimmy's mistress when Alison leaves, is a much tougher character. She stands up to Jimmy and life in the household brightens, but Alison returns, and she and Jimmy come together again. The play ends with them in each other's arms playing their old game of bears and squirrels, a childish fantasy which had been the only level on which their love could function. In the theatre this seemed a painfully good ending, admirable in its irony. The pattern of the play was clearly a circle; we were back where we started and tomorrow the agony would begin all over again. But in a debate after the performance the director, Tony Richardson, denied that this was the meaning. It was a hopeful play, he said. Their relationship had improved, they were playing the game of bears and squirrels with irony and for the last time. The published text confirmed this. Jimmy Porter is supposed to appreciate Alison at the end because she has at last really suffered (she has lost their baby), which is his main criterion for judging people. But this is a false note of happiness. Jimmy will have as much surplus energy as ever, and she has no more strength than before.

There are instances of the same failing in *The Entertainer* (1957), though again its vitality makes it an impressive play.

Archie Rice, a man who is convinced that he can no longer feel anything, tells a long story about a negress whom he once saw singing the blues. He envied her depth of feeling. A few moments later, when the news comes that his son has been killed at Suez, his reaction is to sing some blues himself. It makes a magnificent scene-ending, but the audience was moved because it thought it saw how much Archie Rice was at last moved. If this was Osborne's intention it was a facile and despicable trick. But if, as one hopes, he was writing more seriously, in which case Archie's reaction can reveal only the depths of his tragic artificiality, then the audience should have been appalled, and there was a failure on Osborne's part to fulfil his intention.

With *Luther* (1961) Osborne eliminated these failings and moved with great success to an altogether broader and higher level of playwriting. The play follows Luther's struggles with his sense of guilt and his search for a personal relationship with God—the stirrings of the Protestant conscience. It is in chronicle form, but it is the chronicle of a soul. Historical events come in only where they are directly relevant to Luther's personal development: we see enough of the Peasants' Revolt to appreciate the scar it leaves on Luther but not to understand its historical causes or effects. Critics have complained that the play omits too much, but these omissions are part of its strength. It has the honest and unremitting concentration on a theme which Osborne had previously lacked. Many of the scenes are intensely dramatic—an excellent example is the communal confession in which Luther's uncouth mumblings of guilt stand out against the trivial transgressions so smoothly chanted by the other monks—but Osborne this time avoids all extraneous touches of melodrama. He relies mainly on his strongest weapon—his magnificent ear for spoken prose. This too has become more controlled, more purified. Where *Look Back in Anger* captured one's attention with the clash of cymbals, *Luther* holds it with the lithe and muscular ease of a clarinet. Being Osborne's first imaginative step outside contemporary naturalism, it is a crucial and very hopeful stage in his development.

Arnold Wesker (b. 1932) is in many ways the precise opposite of John Osborne (b. 1929). If Osborne's plays seem like the lively start of a long career, Wesker's highly controlled trilogy is more like its sober ending. The remarkable feature of these three plays is the large quantity of direct moralizing which they contain without sinking, a characteristic which one associates chiefly with a dramatist's last plays.

Chicken Soup with Barley (1958), *Roots* (1959) and *I'm Talking about Jerusalem* (1960) seem at first sight to make up a trilogy only in the very loose sense that each in some way involves Ronnie Kahn. In *Chicken Soup with Barley* he grows up in a family of English Communists. The first scene is set in 1936, the last in 1956, and the play contains excellently the change from idealism to disillusion, from the Spanish Civil War to the Hungarian Uprising, while the characters themselves change from young revolutionaries to middle-aged petty capitalists. Ronnie takes part in *Roots* only as an influence—it is the story of a working-class Norfolk girl who is in love with him. He tries to educate her and fills her with his own ideas, which she relays in a garbled form to her appalled peasant family. Ronnie, despite his idealistic talk of creating a new human being in her, suddenly drops her; but the play ends more hopefully than Wesker's others, for the shock jolts Beatie into finding a voice of her own. In its own harsh and accidental way the 'education' has worked. *I'm Talking about Jerusalem* shows Ronnie's sister and brother-in-law trying to live a William Morris existence by producing handmade furniture in a ramshackle Norfolk house—the family as a Socialist unit. They fail for two reasons. First, opting out of modern industrial society is impracticable; and secondly there is a considerable gap between Dave Simmonds' ideals and his actual way of life. He loses his first job as a carpenter because he takes a bundle of old linoleum belonging to his employer (who would have given it him, had he asked for it) and then denies having done so—a very well-chosen incident, in that it is entirely commonplace and yet significant. This gap between idealism and practice is central to all these three plays, and the sense in which they can lay most claim to the title of trilogy is as three different and, in general, disillusioning experiments in practical Socialism.

Wesker's first play, *The Kitchen* (not given a full production till 1961), dramatizes effectively the hot and noisy routine of work in the kitchen of a large restaurant. This kitchen provides an easy analogy for hectic modern life in an industrial community, but Wesker spoils his play by underlining the moral with literary insistence. One of the chefs tells an excellent story of a bus-driver and a peace march. Its message about people's narrow-mindedness is unmistakable, but the chef goes on to point it out with such literary phrases as '. . . what makes me so sick with terror is . . .'

The Kitchen was based on Wesker's experiences as a pastry-cook, and the character of Ronnie Kahn seems directly auto-biographical. The point has come where Wesker must make a more imaginative act of creation, but he seems to lack the spark which Osborne so fully possesses and it is doubtful whether his drama will be able to develop. *Chicken Soup with Barley* is strangely reminiscent of *Awake and Sing* and there are other obvious similarities between Wesker and Clifford Odets, the Jewish, left-wing, white-hope dramatist of the late thirties whose great promise never materialized.

Osborne and Wesker were the discoveries of the Royal Court Theatre. Two dramatists also emerged from London's other left-wing theatrical stable of the late fifties—Joan Littlewood's Theatre Workshop. These were Brendan Behan (b. 1923) and Shelagh Delaney (b. 1939). Through the new plays which she has chosen to present, and through her method of directing them, Joan Littlewood's name has become associated with a particular style of theatre. It is a loose style, involving countless little scenes, a constant flow of movement on the stage and frequent interruptions of the theatrical illusion. Her approach, even though it has on occasions fossilized into a string of gimmicks, has proved very helpful to actors. It gives them a great vitality on the stage, a freshness and freedom from inhibition. But her influence on her writers may turn out to have been disastrous. Certainly the second plays of both Brendan Behan and Shelagh Delaney conform more nearly to her set style than did their first—in each case to their detriment.

Behan's *The Quare Fellow* (1956) was a *comédie noire* about a prison in which a man is due to be hanged. We never see this 'quare fellow' but his presence in the gaol dominates the whole play. The scenes are sometimes gruesome and often funny, but they are always relevant to the central situation. This gives *The Quare Fellow* a consistency of theme and of character which it shares with Shelagh Delaney's first play. *A Taste of Honey* (1958) is the story of a devil-may-care young girl, the daughter of a brassy near-prostitute; she has a very brief affair with a negro sailor (a black prince, Prince Ossini, in her memory afterwards), becomes pregnant, is protected by a gentle young homosexual, has frequent quarrels with her mother and her mother's bounder of a husband and so drifts on through several months of her life till the curtain falls. The play's merit is its vitality. The brassy mother and her vulgar husband are stock characters and the squabbles between mother and daughter are part of a stock situation; but the freshness of the writing makes this un-important. The dialogue seems to drift in any direction (like Jimmy Porter, the heroine enjoys passing caustic comments on any aspect of modern life), but underneath it a firm pattern of relationships is developed. It is a play in which every character exists only in terms of his or her emotional relationship with the heroine. It is unthinkable, for example, that a humorous plumber should make a brief appearance for the sake of a laugh. It is perhaps this more than anything else which accounts for the tight consistency of texture. The play occupies a bright and almost poetic world of its own.

This is certainly not true of Miss Delaney's second play, *The Lion in Love* (1960), directed in London by a disciple of Miss Littlewood's. Though it centres on an unhappily married couple and their family, there are also a prostitute and her pimp, two gossiping neighbours and even a sandwich-board evangelist, who all drift through the action merely for comic effect. Even worse, random jokes are included which are completely out of context and character. These are faults which have become familiar in the weakest of the new plays presented by Joan Littlewood, and they appear also in Behan's second play.

The Hostage (1959), originally written in Gaelic before *The Quare Fellow* and later adapted for Joan Littlewood, was more commercially successful than *The Quare Fellow* and is admirable entertainment. Superficially it resembles the early O'Casey, in its setting and in its farcical treatment of a tragic subject—the I.R.A. capture of a British soldier as a hostage for an Irish boy sentenced to death. But O'Casey's brilliance lay in the warm reality of his frightened characters caught up in dangerous times. By contrast, Behan's are mere comic ciphers. His bagpipe-playing patriot, his 'camp' homosexual and his Salvation Army woman are mere figures of fun beside Joxer and the Paycock. When the English soldier hears that he will die he protests briefly and then calls for music. He sings a song, 'I am a happy English lad', of which the last verse is:

> I love my dear old Notting Hill
> Wherever I may roam,
> But I wish those bleeding nigger-boys
> Were kicked out and put back home.

This is a cheap topical laugh, and has nothing to do with the Brechtian Alienation Effect. Brecht frequently breaks the theatrical illusion, but he never breaks the mood or meaning of his plays—Behan's song breaks everything to add only an empty joke. It is a symptom of the dangers in the Theatre Workshop style.

In 1951 John Whiting (1917–1963) was given the Arts Theatre Award for a play called *Saint's Day*. That it should have won the prize is a telling comment on the state of English playwriting at the time, because there were over a thousand entries and *Saint's Day* is a singularly bad play. It dealt, in a manner top-heavy with symbol and coincidence, with the subject of a man who disastrously puts his own sense of purpose before personal relationships. Three years later Whiting treated the same theme much more successfully in *Marching Song* (1954). The confusion of *Saint's Day* has gone, and the play reminds one strongly of Betti's *The Burnt Flower Bed*—it moves with easy clarity in a dramatic world which is one step removed from naturalistic reality without ever being out of touch with it. It failed, however, in London; and for several years Whiting seemed to have retired from the theatre. Then in 1961 Peter Hall, the energetic director of the Royal Shakespeare Theatre Company at Stratford-on-Avon, took over a London theatre, the Aldwych, to house his company during the winter. He began to commission new plays, and his first action was to tempt John Whiting to break his silence. The result was *The Devils* (1961), an adaptation of Aldous Huxley's *The Devils of Loudun*. In it Whiting's use of language took a large step forward. With *Marching Song* he had achieved a workmanlike clarity but now he was using words and images with the precision of a jeweller to define character and mood. However, the play has several faults. The comic and the tragic elements tend to dissipate rather than heighten each other, and much of the dialogue seems too carefully planned; but the chief weakness derives directly from the historical story. Grandier, the lascivious priest of Loudun, never actually met Sister Jeanne, the nun who became obsessed with the image of this unobtainable Casanova and whose apparent 'possession' by him led to his execution for sorcery. The core of Whiting's play is the spiritual sufferings of Grandier and the nun, but these are revealed in isolation—Sister Jeanne's mainly in soliloquy, Grandier's in conversation with a symbolic sewer-cleaner. The play therefore lacks the vital moments of confrontation which are essential to drama. It is as though Racine's characters could talk only to their confidants; as though *Hamlet* contained the soliloquies and the grave-digger, but not the scene between Hamlet and his mother.

Robert Bolt (b. 1924) is the least individual of these new playwrights. His plays are characterized by an obvious serious-ness of intention—he tends to wear his theme on his sleeve—and by a smoothly efficient use of symbol and imagery to achieve this intention: otherwise, there is little to suggest that *The Flowering Cherry* (1957), *A Man for all Seasons* and *The Tiger and the Horse* (both 1960) come from the same pen. None of them strikes very deep. *The Flowering Cherry* is perhaps the most success-ful within its own limits. It is the story of a suburban commuter whose dream is of the strong, simple country life. He is convinced that he would become a new man if he could sell everything and farm an apple orchard, but when the opportunity comes he is afraid to take it: his dream was merely a way of not facing his deep inadequacy in his present life. The play's dramatic moments are well contrived—such as the counterpointed ending to Act One, cleverly built up from naturalistic premises—but one is always aware of the contrivance. This is even more true of *The Tiger and the Horse*, a cold, intellectual play whose message, paradoxically, is the importance of emotion. As in Priestley's very similar *The Linden Tree* twelve years earlier, the characters are neatly graded to represent every relevant attitude; but in both plays, as opposed for example to Arthur Miller's, these planned characters fail to transcend the aridity of their conception. Bolt's most widely esteemed play is *A Man for all Seasons*. Since its central character is Sir Thomas More and its subject Integrity, it aims high; but it remains a shallow play with little modern relevance. According to Bolt, More's Roman Catholicism was unassailable and his opposition to the Reformation was therefore a matter of absolute certainty. The play shows Secretary Cromwell's police-state attempts to bully or wheedle More into giving his approval to Henry VIII's divorce, but this surface court-room drama evokes no corresponding struggle in More's soul. As he has no personal doubts and no inclination for the heroic stance, More's fight is one long attempt to avoid execution by a series of legal quibbles. Once again it is very skilfully written and Bolt will undoubtedly produce many more effective plays of a serious, though tame, nature. But he will, I think, turn out to be—in the terms which I defined earlier—a playwright rather than a dramatist.

Another of the authors commissioned by Peter Hall is John Arden (b. 1931). His *Live like Pigs* (1958) is about a family of semi-gipsies who are moved into a council house on a new estate. Their colourfully amoral behaviour outrages the decent neighbours. The play can be taken as an allegory of the rebel in society, but its real appeal comes from the picaresque characters and their richly vivid language. His next play was to have a much more powerful theme.

Sergeant Musgrave's Dance (1960) is too complicated, in the best sense, to be described in a few lines. Its most obvious targets are

the horrors of war and of industrial or colonial exploitation, but
its deepest protest is against any totalitarian method of ending
these injustices. Black Jack Musgrave arrives in a northern town
with three of his soldiers. They pretend to be on a recruiting
mission, but they have brought with them the skeleton of a
comrade, Billy Hicks, whose home town this was. Hicks was
shot in the back while serving in a British Protectorate—the
period is 1880 and the parallel of modern Cyprus is not laboured
—and five innocent natives were killed in the hasty reprisals.
It is disgust at these events which has brought the four soldiers
on their strange mission to this town, but in each of them the
disgust takes a different form. One has become a true pacifist,
wanting only to spread the terrible truth about war; another is
little more than a wild killer, to whom vengeance is a sweet
thought; another is a weak character caught up almost
accidentally by the spirit of the group; and these three are all
dominated by Musgrave himself, a fanatical soldier, obsessed by
the idea of order and by a savage logic of reprisals. If five natives
died as a reprisal for Billy Hicks, he argues, by simple mathematics twenty-five people must die as a reprisal for those five. And
these twenty-five must be men like the Priest or the Mayor or
the merchants, the men responsible, in his opinion, for the war.
He has come to demand, as the only way towards ultimate
peace, a bloody revolution which will turn war back on the
warmongers. The terrible flaw in his dogmatic attitude first
appears when the soldiers kill the weakest of their number
because he tries to 'betray the cause' by going off with a girl.
Already the seeds of what Musgrave opposes are appearing in
his own camp. *Sergeant Musgrave's Dance* is more deeply thoughtful
than any other new British play and the thought is fully dramatized. Arden's language, characters and scenes burst with a
harsh life which seems entirely spontaneous. There is no
impression, as there is with Bolt, of an idea which has been
neatly clothed with drama and which can therefore, just as
neatly, be undressed again. The play has, however, one major
defect—Arden waits too long before giving the audience any
clear idea of the real nature of the soldiers' mission. This
obscurity was undoubtedly the cause of the play's failure in

London, because an audience is unable to appreciate the subtle differences between the four soldiers until it knows what they have in common. But this flaw, though it has a large effect on the play's impact, is in itself only a small technical misjudgement. It in no way invalidates the complex talent revealed in the play.

The Birthday Party (1958) was the first play by Harold Pinter, who was born in 1930. Deriving to some extent from Ionesco, it is a neurotic study of the pressure towards conformity brought to bear on a second-rate young artist who has opted out of material success and responsibility. Two mysterious visitors arrive to remove Stanley from the boarding-house where he is sponging off a warm-hearted and mothering landlady. Between them they represent most aspects of authority. Goldberg, an upper-class Jew, speaks a language which is a brilliant mixture of Uncle Barney and the old school tie, and his henchman, McCann, is a fanatical Catholic. Together they use all the tactics of third-degree interrogation on the miserable Stanley until finally they break him down, dress him up in a respectable dark suit and take him away. The language of the play is, at its best, a superb distillation of ordinary conversation, both in rhythm and content.

The Birthday Party can be criticized for being derivative— besides Ionesco, Beckett is a clear influence—but with *The Caretaker* (1960) Pinter moved towards his own individual form of theatre. It is a much more straightforward play than *The Birthday Party*. Instead of a heightened allegory of a very subjective experience, it presents a simple relationship between three men —an old tramp and the two brothers whom he plays off against each other because either of them might be able to give him a bed and a job. The language is still the purest essence of the twists and turns of ordinary conversation (see page 73), but, in keeping with its subject-matter, it avoids the formal extremes of *The Birthday Party*.

Even so, traces of the more intellectual approach of *The Birthday Party* remain (the elder brother, Mick, for example, sometimes seems more like an idea than a person, as were Goldberg and McCann), and the play contains misleading hints that the surface drama may be an allegory of some deeper meaning. It has even been suggested that it is a study of schizophrenia, the brothers being the two halves of one person. Pinter has denied that he had any such intention, and schizophrenia is not, in any case, a neat Jekyll and Hyde state of affairs. Certainly the play stands best on the simplest level. Its chief irony, which could perhaps be called its 'point', is that the only character to show any signs of charity is Aston, the 'mentally deranged' brother who has undergone shock treatment of the brain—an operation which has the effect of lessening a man's will and ambition.

Stray and unconnected overtones are a danger in Harold Pinter's work. An early one-act play, *A Slight Ache*, abounded in them—disastrously. In *The Birthday Party* the overtones were controlled, given their own specific limits, and made effective. *The Caretaker*, almost free of them, could be called distilled naturalism—a style of theatre which, it seems, can make dramatic the simplest relationships not so much by giving them a plot as by giving them a form.

Something about a book of this sort demands that it should end with a look forward, but, fortunately, the first rule of oracles is brevity. To the question 'Which way will the theatre of the next decade develop?' one can answer only by extending observation into wish-fulfilment. My own confident hope is that the influence of Beckett will continue to be felt in the sphere of language: already dramatists as different as John Whiting and Harold Pinter are making use of the ripple of his loosely patterned dialogue. But the most useful general influence on contemporary theatre seems likely to be Brecht's. Friedrich Dürrenmatt, Max Frisch and John Arden all represent different developments of his theatre, and now the new English playwrights show signs of wanting to increase the generality, the moral significance, of their plays. Osborne has written *Luther*, Wesker is planning a play about the life of Christ, Shelagh Delaney one about fifteenth-century Derby. If such plays are to avoid being mere costume dramas, it is Brecht's example which will be needed. Pirandello has been the most

influential modern dramatist since the First World War. I
believe and hope that the next twenty years of theatre will be
influenced as strongly by Brecht: not by his theories and
politics, but by his far more important qualities—his intelligence, his poetic clarity, his moral concern and, above all, his
humanity.

Notes

[1] In an interview in *Cambridge Opinion 21*, 1960.

[2] Arthur Miller, Preface to *Collected Plays*, Cresset Press, 1958.

[3] Joseph Gregor, in *Theatre in a Changing Europe*, ed. T. Dickinson, Putnam, 1938.

[4] Translated by Hermann Scheffauer; Kaiser, *Gas*, Chapman and Dodd, 1924.

[5] Translated by Ashley Dukes; Toller, *Seven Plays*, Bodley Head, 1935.

[6] Translated by Edward Crankshaw; Toller, *Seven Plays*, Bodley Head, 1935.

[7] Translated by Hermann Scheffauer; Kaiser, *Gas*, Chapman and Dodd, 1924.

[8] Translated by Ashley Dukes; Kaiser, *From Morn till Midnight*, Henderson's, 1922.

[9] Quoted by Willson Whitman, *Bread and Circuses*, O.U.P., 1937.

[10] Translated by Martin Esslin, in *Brecht, a Choice of Evils*, Eyre and Spottiswoode, 1960.

[11] Translated by Henry Reed; Ugo Betti, *Three Plays*, Gollancz, 1956.

[12] Translated by Christopher Fry; Jean Giraudoux, *Tiger at the Gates*, Methuen, 1955.

[13] Quoted and translated by Martin Esslin, *Brecht, a Choice of Evils*, Eyre and Spottiswoode, 1960.

[14] Translated by Eric and Maja Bentley; Brecht, *Parables for the Theatre*, Grove Press, 1948.

[15] Translated by James Graham-Lujan and Richard L. O'Connell; Lorca, *Three Tragedies*, New Directions, 1947.

[16] T. S. Eliot, *Poetry and Drama*, Theodore Spencer Lecture, Harvard, 1950.

[17] Translated by James Graham-Lujan and Richard L. O'Connell; Lorca, *Three Tragedies*, New Directions, 1947.

[18] Ibid.

[19] *Observer*, October 16, 1960.

[20] Translated by Paul Selver; J. and K. Čapek, 'And so ad Infinitum', O.U.P., 1923.

[21] T. S. Eliot, Poetry and Drama, Theodore Spencer Lecture, Harvard, 1950.

[22] Translated by Arthur Livingston; Pirandello, Each In Own Way, and other plays, Dutton, 1925.

[23] Translated by Arthur Livingston; Naked Masks (five plays by Pirandello, ed. Eric Bentley), Dutton, 1952.

[24] Quoted and translated by Lander MacClintock, The Age of Pirandello, Indiana University Studies, 1951.

[25] Brecht, Theaterarbeit, quoted and translated by John Willett, The Theatre of Bertolt Brecht, Methuen, 1959.

[26] Translated by Eric and Maja Bentley; Brecht, Parables for the Theatre, Grove Press, 1948.

[27] Translated by Desmond Vesey; Brecht, Plays, Vol. 1, Methuen, 1960.

[28] Brecht to his actors, in conversation; quoted by K. Rueliche, Sinn und Form, 1957, translated by Martin Esslin, Brecht, a Choice of Evils, Eyre and Spottiswoode, 1960.

[29] Ronald Gray, Brecht, Writers and Critics Series, Oliver and Boyd, 1961.

[30] Translated by Desmond Vesey; Brecht, Plays, Vol. 1, Methuen, 1960.

[31] Quoted and translated by Donald Inskip, The Makings of a Dramatist, O.U.P., 1958.

[32] Translated by Christopher Fry; Giraudoux, Tiger at the Gates, Methuen, 1955.

[33] Translated by Christopher Fry; Giraudoux, Duel of Angels, Methuen, 1958.

[34] Tennessee Williams, Introduction to Camino Real in Four Plays, Secker and Warburg, 1956.

[35] Eric Bentley, What is Theatre?, Dobson, 1957.

[36] Joseph Wood Krutch, The American Drama since 1918, Thames and Hudson, 1958.

[37] Arthur Miller, Preface to Collected Plays, Cresset Press, 1958.

Index

The dates represent a play's first production or publication. In the few cases, however, where a play was not produced or published for more than four years after its completion—as with some of Claudel, O'Neill and Brecht—I have instead given the date of its completion.